CCEA | GCSE

FRENCH VOCABULARY BOOK 3

School Life, Studies & the World of Work

COLOURPOINT
EDUCATIONAL

© Diarmuid Brittain and Colourpoint Creative Ltd 2022

ISBN: 978 1 78073 288 6

First Edition
First impression

Layout and design: April Sky Design
Printed by: GPS Colour Graphics Ltd, Belfast

The Author

Diarmuid Brittain taught French for 26 years at Grosvenor Grammar School, Belfast. He is also an A level French Examiner for an awarding body.

He lives with his wife and three children in Belfast and remains a Francophile through and through.

This book has borrowed inspiration from hundreds of pupils over the years and it is dedicated to each and every language student and teacher that has graced the doors of Grosvenor Grammar School.

COLOURPOINT EDUCATIONAL

Colourpoint Educational
An imprint of Colourpoint Creative Ltd
Colourpoint House
Jubilee Business Park
21 Jubilee Road
Newtownards
County Down
Northern Ireland
BT23 4YH

Tel: 028 9182 0505
E-mail: sales@colourpoint.co.uk
Website: www.colourpoint.co.uk

This book has been written to help students preparing for the GCSE French specification from CCEA. While Colourpoint Educational and the author have taken every care in its production, we are not able to guarantee that the book is completely error-free. Additionally, while the book has been written to closely match the CCEA specification, it is the responsibility of each candidate to satisfy themselves that they have fully met the requirements of the CCEA specification prior to sitting an exam set by that body. For this reason, and because specifications change with time, we strongly advise every candidate to avail of a qualified teacher and to check the contents of the most recent specification for themselves prior to the exam. Colourpoint Educational therefore cannot be held responsible for any errors or omissions in this book or any consequences thereof.

Contents

Introduction

This is one of four books that form a resource for English-speaking students of French and which seeks to promote **student-led vocabulary acquisition**. It is designed to **promote independent learning** and **free up teacher time**. While it is tailored for GCSE students, it is a powerful resource for all English-speaking students of French.

What do the books cover?

Various GCSE French syllabi (CCEA, WJEC, Edexcel, AQA, OCR) have common vocabulary lists. While this resource makes specific reference to the CCEA specification, it covers the vocabulary listed in all these syllabi and can be used with all of them.

The resource is divided into four books, the first three of which cover the three areas of core vocabulary as presented in the GCSE syllabi:
1. Identity, Lifestyle and Culture
2. Local, National, International and Global Areas of Interest
3. School Life, Studies and the World of Work (this book)

The resource is completed by a fourth book:
4. Verbs, Conjunctions and Other Useful Phrases, which includes an alphabetical list of the most common verbs in French, as well as a list of common connectors, *la Colle Française* (French glue).

Why these books?

- These books are designed to be used independently by students.
- Traditionally, students have been given lists of vocabulary to learn without pronunciation guides and without *aide-mémoires*. With these books, teachers can hand vocabulary learning over to their students, giving the teacher more time to focus on the challenging grammar that requires teacher-led pedagogy.
- Research shows that pupils prefer to learn from hard copies.
- Pupils can have a sense of ownership of this a resource because they can annotate it.
- The most recent GCSE CCEA specification (first examined in 2017) places more emphasis on Listening and Reading, demanding a higher level of vocabulary acquisition.
- This resource can be used independently by students from Year 8 onwards, building over five years to GCSE success. This is particularly useful for schools that need to use remote learning from time to time.

What is the structure of this book?

The vocabulary in the book is presented in the same order as it is presented in the CCEA GCSE syllabus, i.e. in alphabetical order by the English meaning.

Each word has a **pronunciation guide**. The benefits of this are the following:

- Learners can check their pronunciation of the word.
- Learners can test understanding from looking only at the pronunciation guide, thereby improving their listening skills.
- Learners can test themselves on how to write – in correct French – the phonetically described word, thereby improving the accuracy of their writing.
- Learners can work in pairs to test each other orally from English to French and/or French to English.

Most words also have an ***aide-mémoire***. *Aide-mémoire* is French for 'memory aid'. People often struggle under the burden of learning vocabulary, and take little pleasure from the task.

It is the author's belief that if a student can find links between their own language and a foreign one, it makes the process of vocabulary acquisition more of a journey of discovery than a drudgery, and importantly, it allows the learner to hook the foreign words onto words that have already been assimilated in their brain.

The author likes to work with the premise 'words can make you laugh!' There are a number of attempts to be humorous throughout the book, in an effort to link works to the mind of the student. Learners may describe these attempts as 'dad jokes' – but the author believes that learners secretly like them!

The book also includes sections entitled **Practise!** These allow students to practise what they have learned, embedding their learning. Teachers will also find these sections useful in order to set homework or cover work.

What are the tick boxes for?

Each word has three tick boxes. These are provided in order to give the student a way to track their progress and organise their learning. The author suggests the following approach, though you can use whatever method works for you:

- Tick the first box when you have learned the word for the first time. When you are organising your revision use this tick to indicate to yourself what you have covered.
- When you come back later to check that you have retained the word, you can tick the second box.
- By the time you go in to your GCSE exams, you should have been able to tick the third box, to show that you have embedded that word in your brain.

Abbreviations

The book uses the following abbreviations:

(m)	masculine	e.g. *Un garçon*, a boy
(f)	feminine	e.g. *Une fille*, a girl
(m/f)	masculine or feminine	e.g. *Un/une professeur*, a teacher
(mpl)	masculine plural	e.g. *Des garçons*, (some) boys
(fpl)	feminine plural	e.g. *Des filles*, (some) girls

1. Mes études
(My studies)

Word or phrase	Pronunciation guide	Aide-mémoire	English meaning	Check		
Dessin (m)	dess-ah	Design	Art			
Biologie (f)	bee-all-oh-zhee		Biology			
L'étude (f) du commerce	lay-tood du com-airse	The 'é' replaces 's', so 'stude' – study. Commerce means trade, means business.	Business Studies			
Chimie (f)	she-mee	Careful, it's ch**i**, not che-mie	Chemistry			
Civilisation (f)	see-vee-lee-zass-yaw		Citizenship			
Technologie (f)	tek-nall-low-zhee		Design Technology			
Art (m) dramatique	aarh drama-teek	Dramatic art	Drama			
Économie (f)	ay-kon-omee		Economics			
Anglais (m)	awn-glay	Angl is like **Engl**-ish	English			
Sciences Vie Terre (fpl)	see-awse-vee-tair	Vie – vivid (bright), vivacious (full of life). Terre – territory, ground, earth.	Environment studies			
Langues (fpl) étrangères	lawng ay-trawn-zhair	'é' replaces 's' at the start of a word. Stranger, strange, foreign.	Foreign languages			
Français (m)	fraw-say		French			
Sport (m)	spore		Games			
Géographie (f)	zhay-oh		Geography			
Allemand (m)	aal-maw	It's got 'man' in it	German			
Gymnastique (f)	zheem-nass-teek		Gymnastics			
Histoire (f)	east-wire		History			
Histoire-géo (f)	east-wire zhay-oh		History/Geography			
Informatique (f)	ah-for-mat-eek	Information technology	IT			
Irlandais (m)	eer-lawn-day		Irish			
Italien (m)	ee-taahl-yeah		Italian			
Instruction (f) civique	ah-strook-see-yaw see-veek		LLW, Citizenship			
Maths (fpl)	mat		Maths			
L'étude (f) des médias	lay-tood day may-dee-ah	é replaces an 's' at the start	Media studies			
Langues (fpl) vivantes	lawng vee-vawnt	Langue – language. Vivantes – vibrant, vivid, vivacious. Living, modern languages.	Modern languages			
Musique (f)	moo-zeek		Music			
L'EPS (f)	leuh pay ess	Education Physique Sportive	PE			
Education (f) physique	ay-doo-kass-yaw fee-zeek		PE			
Philosophie (f)	fee-law-soh-fee		Philosophy			
Physique (f)	fee-zeek		Physics			

Word or phrase	Pronunciation guide	Aide-mémoire	English meaning	Check
Psychologie (f)	see-coll-oh-zhee		Psychology	
Religion (f)	rel-ee-zhaw		RE/RS	
Sociologie (f)	soh-see-all-oh-zhee		Sociology	
Espagnol (m)	ess pan yall	It's got the 'spa' of **Spa**nish	Spanish	
Matière (f)	matty-air	Raw matter, subject matter: what school consists of.	Subject (school)	
Vocabulaire (m)	voh-kah-boo-lair		Vocabulary	
Gallois (m)	gahl-wah	W**al**es, -ois is the ending for many languages: sued-ois, dan-ois, g**all**-ois.	Welsh	

Practise!

1. Fais une liste de tes matières préférées en commençant avec ta préférée.
   (*Make a list of your favourite subjects, in French, starting with your favourite.*)

   _____

   _____

   _____

   _____

2. Fais une liste des matières que tu aimerais peut-être faire pour les A levels.
   (*Make a list of subjects that you might like to do for A level.*)

   _____

   _____

   _____

   _____

3. Sur une échelle mondiale, fais une liste en ordre de ce que tu penses être des langues d'école, de la plus populaire à la moins populaire. (*On a worldwide scale, list in order what you think are the most popular school-taught languages, from the most popular to the least popular.*)

   1. _____

   2. _____

   3. _____

   4. _____

4. Quelles sont les matières qu'on n'étudie pas ici mais qui sont étudiées en France?
   (*Which are the subjects that we do not study here but that are studied in France?*)

   _____

   _____

   _____

   _____

2. La vie scolaire
[School life]

Word or phrase	Pronunciation guide	Aide-mémoire	English meaning	Check		
Absent(e/s) (adj)	ab-saw (sawnt)		Absent			
Le CDI	say-day-ooh	Centre de Documentation et d'Information	Academic information centre			
Réponse (f)	ray-pawn-seuh	Response	Answer			
Salle d'assemblée	saal dass awm-blay	Salle – salon – room (hall) for Assembly	Assembly hall			
Bac(calauréat) (m)	bak(ah-lore-ay-ah)		Baccalaureate (A level equivalent)			
Bâtiments (mpl)	bat-ee-maw	^ denotes next letter, 's', Link therefore from bâtiment to bastion, a fort, a building.	Buildings			
Récréation/ récré (f)	ray-kray-ass-yaw/ ray-kray	Time for recreation	Break			
Brevet (m)	breuh-vay		Brevet (GCSE equivalent)			
Cantine (f)	cawn-teen		Cantine			
Concierge (m/f)	caw-see-air-zheuh	The word concierge is used in English. It also has the same starting letter.	Caretaker			
Vestiaires (mpl)	vest-ee-air	Strip down to your **vest** in the changing room	Changing room			
Chorale (f)	koh-raahl	Choral evensong carried out by the **choir**	Choir			
Cours (m)	kouhr	A **cours**e in university is a class in a subject. A **cours**e of study.	Class			
Salle (f) de classe	sal-deuh-klahss	**Class**e **sal**on, saloon, room	Classroom			
Salle (f) commune	saal cawm-oon	Commune common, **sal**on, saloon, room	Common room			
Couloirs (mpl)	koul-wire	A raspberry **coul**is is a sauce, it flows, people flow in a **co**rrid**or**	Corridors			
Remplaçant (e/s)	rawm-plahss-awe(awnt)	A **re**m**plac**er	Cover/supply teacher			
Retenue (f)	reuh-teuh-noo	If you are retained, you are held back, in detention	Detention			
Éducation (f)	ay-doo-kass-yaw		Education			
Examen (m)	egg-zah-mah	Pronounced 'eczema', like the skin disease, which is brought on by stress	Examination			
Exercice (m)	eks-air-seese		Exercise/practice			
Expérience (f)	eks-pay-ree-oss	A false friend here. An experience is an experiment.	Experiment			
Seconde (f)	seuh-gawnd	1st Yr is 6th Yr, **2nd is 5th**, 3rd is 4th, 4th is 3rd, 5th is 2nd, 6th is 1st, U6 is Terminale	Fifth year (year 11/12)			
Sixième (f)	see-zee-em	**1st Yr is 6th** Yr, 2nd is 5th, 3rd is 4th, 4th is 3rd, 5th is 2nd, 6th is 1st, U6 is Terminale	First year (year 7/8)			

Word or phrase	Pronunciation guide	Aide-mémoire	English meaning	Check
Troisième (f)	tr-wah-zee-em	1st Yr is 6th Yr, 2nd is 5th, **3rd is 4th**, 4th is 3rd, 5th is 2nd, 6th is 1st, U6 is Terminale	Fourth year (year 10/11)	
Fort(e/s) en	foar/foart awe	A fort is strong, a stronghold. If you are strong in a subject you are good at it.	Good (at a subject)	
Gymnase (m)	zheem-nazz		Gym	
Directeur(trice)	dee-rek-teuhr(treese)		Headteacher (general)	
Principal(e)	prah-see-pal		Headteacher (secondary 11-15)	
Proviseur	proh-vee-zehur	Su**pervisor**	Headteacher (secondary 15-18)	
Bureau (m) du proviseur	boo-roh doo pro-vee-zeuhr	Bureau de change, office to change money. Proviseur – provides leadership	Head teacher's office (15-18)	
Devoirs (mpl)	deuh-vwaahr	Devoir means 'to have to'. You have to do your homework. It's your **d**uty.	Homework	
Salle (f) d'informatique	sahl dahl four-mat-eek	**Sal**on for **informati**on technology	ICT suite	
Leçon (f)	leuh-saw		Lesson	
Bibliothèque (f)	beeb-leah-oh-tec	Bible is a book found here	Library	
Première (f) année	prem-ee-air ah-nay	1st is 6th, 2nd is 5th, 3rd is 4th, 4th is 3rd, 5th is 2nd, **L6th is première**, U6 is Terminale	Lower sixth (year 13)	
L'heure (f) du déjeuner	leuhr-doo-day-zheunay	The hour (heure) of breaking fast. Jeûner – to fast, 'dé' reverses the verb, breaks it.	Lunchtime	
Cour (f) de récréation	couhr	**Cour**tyard of recreation, play	Playground	
Poésie (f)	Po-ay-zee		Poetry	
Permanence (f)	pair-ma-nawse	This is a permanent study area, it doesn't change to have another purpose	Private study area	
Élève (m/f)	ay-lev	You bring up, or **elev**ate your children. Teachers eleve-ate their pupils.	Pupil	
accueil (m)	ah-koo-ay	'Acc' come on in! Accueillir, the verb 'to welcome', a reception.	Reception	
Bulletin (m) scolaire	Boo-leuh-tah skoh-lair	A news bulletin is a report. Scolaire describes school.	Report	
Local (m) / locaux (mpl)	loh-cal / loh-coh	A local hall is a room	Room	
École (f)	ay-koll	'é' at start of word replaces 's' – school	School	
Salle (f) de sports	sahl-deuh-spore	**Sal**on of sports	Sports hall	
Terrains (mpl) de sport	tair-ah-deuh-spore	Terrain, territory, ground	Sports pitches	
Salle (f) des profs	sahl-day-prof	**Sal**on of professors (teachers)	Staff room	
Rentrée (f)	rawn-tray	The **ret**ur**nee**s are the people who go back	Start of the school year	

Word or phrase	Pronunciation guide	Aide-mémoire	English meaning	Check
Cinquième (f)	sank-ee-em	1st Yr is 6th Yr, **2nd is 5th**, 3rd is 4th, 4th is 3rd, 5th is 2nd, 6th is 1st, U6 is Terminale	Second year (year 8/9)	
Collège (m)	Kaw-leh-zheuh	College, like school	Secondary school, (11-15yrs)	
Lycée (m)	Lee-say	If you are awarded your **license** (**lycee**nse) you are a senior pupil who has passed	Secondary school (16-18yrs)	
Scène (f)	sen	Scene where the action takes place in a play	Stage	
Trimestre (m)	Tree-mess-treuh	Trimester is an American word for a term	Term	
Contrôle (m)	Kawn-troll	A control experiment evaluates progress, like a test	Test	
Uniforme (m)	Ooh-nee-form		Uniform	
Université (f)	Ooh-nee-vair-see-tay		University	
Étudiant(e/s) (m/f)	Ay-too-dee-aw/ awnt	'é' replaces 's' at the start of a word	Student	
Études (fpl)	Ay-tood	'é' replaces 's' at the start of a word	Studies	
Prof(esseur) (m/f)	Proh-fess-euhr	A professor is a teacher	Teacher	
Équipe (f)	Ay-keep	The members of a team are the pieces of **equip**m**e**nt of that team	Team	
Quatrième (f)	Kat-ree-em	1st yr is 6th yr, 2nd is 5th, **3rd is 4th**, 4th is 3rd, 5th is 2nd, 6th is 1st, U6 is Terminale	Third year (year 9/10)	
Emploi du temps (m)	Awm-plwah-doo-taw	Employ your time, how you employ time is a timetable	Timetable	
Toilettes (fpl)/ WC (mpl)	twah-let	**W**ater **C**loset	Toilets	
Terminale (f)	Tair-mee-nahl	1st Yr is 6th Yr, 2nd is 5th, 3rd is 4th, 4th is 3rd, 5th is 2nd, 6th is 1st, **U6 is Terminale**	Upper sixth (year 13/14)	
Faible(s)/ mauvais(e/s)	Feb-leuh/ moh-vay(vays)	Feeble is weak, **f**ai**ble**. Mauvais – 'ma' is linked to mal which is a bad prefix, e.g. malignant, malicious, malnourished.	Weak (at a subject)	
Fiche (f) de travail	Feesh deuh trav-eye	Travail – trial, tribulation, to do with work. Fiche – pin your worksheet on a dead **fiche**.	Worksheet	

Practise!

Find the twelve most difficult words or phrases to remember from this large section and list them below in French and English:

1. _____ _____ 2. _____ _____

3. _____ _____ 4. _____ _____

5. _____ _____ 6. _____ _____

7. _____ _____ 8. _____ _____

9. _____ _____ 10. _____ _____

11. _____ _____ 12. _____ _____

3. La salle de classe
[The classroom]

Word or phrase	Pronunciation guide	Aide-mémoire	English meaning	Check
Tableau (m) noir	tah-bloh nwaarh	A **table** top is like a board, **n**oir, **n**egro, black	Blackboard	
Livre (m)	lee-vreuh	**Lever** arch files hold books. **Lit**eratu**re**.	Book	
Bâtiments (mpl)	bat-ee-maw	^ says that the next letter would be 's', like bastion, a fort, a building	Buildings	
Calculette (f)	kahl-koo-let	A little **calcul**ator (-ette, a little …)	Calculator	
Couloir (m)	kouh-lwaahr	A raspberry **coul**is is a sauce, it flows, people flow in a **corridor**	Corridor	
Pupitre (f)	poo-pee-treuh	**Pupi**ls sit at desks	Desk	
Dictionnaire (m)	deeks-yawn-air		Dictionary	
Gomme (f)	gawm	**Gum** boots are rubber boots, gum, gomme, rubber, eraser	Eraser/rubber	
Cahier (m)	kah-yay	'**Ca**roline, **Hi**, I am **Er**ic'. Shall we **book** some **exercise**?	Exercise book	
Laboratoire (m)	lah-boh-rat-wire		Laboratory	
Langue (f)	lawng	Langue, linguist, language	Language	
Leçon (f)	leuh-saw		Lesson	
Feutre (m)	feuh-treuh	**Fel**t tipped	Marker/felt-tip	
Stylo (m)	stee-loh	A stylus is used to trace a line	Pen	
Crayon (m)	kray-awe	A pencil with colour in Eng. Just a pencil in Fr.	Pencil	
Trousse (f)	trouhss	Take a **trouser** leg, close it at both ends, attach a zip, it's a pencil case	Pencil case	
Instituteur(s)/ institutrice(s)	ah-stee-too-teuhr/ ah-stee-too-treese	A primary school is an institute. An instituter works there.	Primary school teacher	
Maître(s)/ maîtresse(s)	met-reuh/ met-ress	A **ma**s**ter** is an old word for a primary teacher	Primary school teacher	
Projecteur	proh-zhek-teur		Overhead projector	
Règle (f)	rehg-leuh	If you **reg**ula**te** the way things happen, you rule, you are the ruler	Ruler	
Ciseaux (mpl)	see-zoh		Scissors	
Taille-crayon (m)	tye-kray-yaw	'Tailler' is 'to cut', gives us 'tailor' cutter of cloth. Here we cut the crayon.	Sharpener	
Professeur (m/f)	proh-fess-euhr	Professors are teachers	Teacher	
Tableau (m) intéractif	tah-bloh ah-tair-ak-teef	An interactive table-top	Whiteboard	

Practise!

On a separate sheet of paper, draw a classroom including as many of the items above as possible. Label the items correctly in French.

4. Les activités extra-scolaires
(Extra-curricular activities)

Word or phrase	Pronunciation guide	Aide-mémoire	English meaning	Check
Activité (f)	ak-tee-vee-tay		Activity	
Athlétisme (m)	at-lay-tees-meuh		Athletics	
Badminton (m)	bad-meen-ton		Badminton	
Basketball (m)	bass-ket-ball		Basketball	
Devenir membre d'un club	deuh-veuh-neer mawm-breuh dah klub	De**ven**ir, **ven**ir, **ven**ue – a place you come to. French, decome. English, become.	Become a member of a club	
Boxe (f)	box		Boxing	
Échecs (mpl)	ay-shek	Looks a bit like chess, échecs. Common letters are: **echs**.	Chess	
Clarinette (f)	klah-ree-net		Clarinet	
Club (m)	klub		Club	
Informatique (f)	ah-for-mat-eek	**Informat**ion technology	Computing	
Cyclisme (m)	see-klees-meuh		Cycling	
Art (m) dramatique	aahr-drah		Drama	
Passionnant (e/s)	pass-yawn-aw	Passionate about something is excited about something	Exciting	
Pêche (f)	pesh	**P**is**ce**s (zodiac sign for fish). **P**os**e**idon, Greek sea god.	Fishing	
Flûte (f)	floot		Flute	
Amusant(e/s)	ah-moo-zaw		Fun	
Jeu (m)	zheuh	**Jeu** comes from jouer, to play. Also the **joy** of playing. Glentoran football team slogan: 'le jeu avant tout' ('the game before all').	Game	
Salle de jeux (f)	sahl-deuh-zheuh	Salle, salon. Salon is a room, jeux are game**s**, from jouer, to play. **x** is a plural.	Games room	
Guitare (f)	gee-taarh		Guitar	
Gymnastique (f)	zheem-nast-eek		Gymastics	
Passetemps (m)	pass-taw	Pastime, passtemps	Hobby	
Club (m) de hockey	klub deuh ock-ay		Hockey club	
Équitation (f)	ay-kee-tass-yaw	**Equ**e**stria**n, equine, to do with horses	Horse-riding	
Judo (m)	zhooh-doh		Judo	
Karate (m)	kah-rah-tay		Karate	
Arts (mpl) martiaux	aarh mahr-see-yoh	**x** is plural here	Martial arts	
Orchestre (m)	oar-kess-treuh		Orchestra	

Word or phrase	Pronunciation guide	Aide-mémoire	English meaning	Check
Piano (m)	pee-ah-noh		Piano	
Pièce (f) de théâtre	pee-yes deuh tay-at-reuh	A piece of theatre is a sketch or a play	Play	
Entraînement de rugby	awn-tren-maw deuh rug-bee	En**train**ement	Rugby training	
Course (f) à pied	koarse-ah-pee-yay	A race course, where you race on foot, run. Pied, **ped**estrian, **pod**iatry, foot.	Running	
Couture (f)	kouh-toohr	**Co**u**t**ure is to do with **cut**ting fabric, sewing	Sewing	
Chanter dans la chorale	shawn-tay daw soon koh-rahl	Chanting in the choral	Singing in the choir	
Skate (m)	skayt		Skateboarding	
Salle (f) de sports	sahl deuh spore	Salle, salon, room or hall	Sports hall	
Natation (f)	nah-tass-yaw	**Na**vy, **na**utical. To do with water, swimming.	Swimming	
Tennis (m)	ten-neese		Tennis	
Jeux (mpl) vidéo	zheuh-vee-day-oh	**Jeu** comes from jouer, to play. Also the **joy** of playing. **x** is plural, game**s**.	Video-games	
Volley (m)	vawl-ay	Lost the ball, retained the volley.	Volleyball	

Practise!

Read the following descriptions and try to match them up to one of the words above. Write the appropriate word in French and in English.

1. C'est une activité japonaise mais ce n'est pas un sport olympique.

   _____

2. C'est un sport qui implique les personnes et les chevaux.

   _____

3. Ce n'est pas un sport. C'est une activité de grand groupe où il y a de la musique.

   _____

4. C'est un sport qu'on fait sur les rivières, les lacs et la mer.

   _____

5. C'est un instrument de musique qui est très grand et pas portable.

   _____

6. C'est un sport qui se pratique dans une piscine.

   _____

7. Ce n'est pas un sport, Les français sont célèbres pour cette activité liée à la mode.

   _____

8. Pour pouvoir jouer à ce sport, il est bien d'être très grand.

   _____

9. Pour participer à ce sport, il faut être très souple.

_____

10. C'est une activité qu'on aime faire pendant son temps libre.

_____

11. Ce n'est pas un sport. Les gens y participent dans une salle de théâtre.

_____

12. Ce n'est pas un sport physiquement exigeant. Ça se fait devant un écran.

_____

13. C'est un sport et c'est aussi un mode de transport.

_____

14. C'est un sport qui se fait avec les petites balles normalement jaunes.

_____

15. Il est nécessaire de faire ceci si on veut être fort en rugby.

_____

16. On participe à ces activités parce que c'est ...

_____

17. Normalement, pour faire cette activité, on a besoin d'un ordinateur.

_____

18. C'est un sport où deux personnes se battent avec les gants sur les mains.

_____

19. Des exemples de cette activité sont le saut en hauteur et le saut en longueur.

_____

20. C'est un sport où on doit penser bien fort avant de jouer.

_____

5. Les emplois à temps partiel
[Part-time jobs]

Word or phrase	Pronunciation guide	Aide-mémoire	English meaning	Check
Annonce (f)	ah-nawnse	An **anno**un**ce**ment to let people know	Ad (in a news-paper, online)	
S'adresser à	sah-dress-ay ah	To **ad**d**ress** oneself to	Address, to address oneself to	
Publicité (f) une	po-blee-see-tay	Give **publicit**y to something to advertise it	Advertisement	
Publicité (f) la (la pub)	po-blee-see-tay	Give **publicit**y to something to advertise it	Advertising/ advertisement	
Ambition (f)	awm-beese-yaw		Ambition	
Poser (v) sa candidature	po-zay sah kon-dee-dah-toohr	To **pos**ition one's candidacy	Apply	
Faire une demande pour	fair oon deuh-mawnd pouhr	Make a demand for to work. E.g. 'Faire une demande pour travailler chez Tesco'.	Apply	
Candidat/ Candidate (m/f)	kon-dee-dah/ kon-dee-dat	A candidate for the job	Applicant	
Mal payé(e/s)	mahl pay-yay	Mal – bad, **mal**icious, **mal**aria, **mal**practice	Badly paid	
Chef (m/f)	sheff	Chief	Boss	
Patron/ Patronne (m/f)	pah-traw/ pah-trawn	Prince Charles, the Patron of the Duke of Edinburgh scheme. The boss. The patron saint of Ireland is St Patrick. The boss saint!	Boss	
Commerce (m)	kaw-mairse	Commerce is about trading is about business	Business	
Affaires commerciales (fpl)	ah-fair kaw-mair-see-ahl	Commercial affairs are business affairs	Business	
Occupé(e/s)	awe-koo-pay	Occupied, like the toilet, someone is busy in there	Busy	
Conseiller/ conseillère d'orientation (m/f)	kaw-say-yay /kaw-sy-yair dore-ee-awn-tass-yaw	Orientation is the direction in which you wish to travel professionally. This person is a counsellor on this topic, on your career direction.	Careers advisor	
Caissier/ caissière (m/f)	kess-ee-yay/ kess-ee-yair	**Cas**h**ier**	Cashier	
Collègue (m/f)	koll-ehg		Colleague	
Rêve (m)	rev	Lost in **revery** – one is lost in daydreaming	Dream	
Expérience (f)	eks-pay-ree-awsse		Experience	
Remplir un formulaire	rom-pleer ah for-moo-lair	Remplir, **repl**en**i**sh, fill. A **form**ulaire.	Fill in a form	
Entreprise (f)	awn-treuh-preeze	Enterprise is associated with business. Run by an entrepreneur.	Firm (business)	
Avenir (m)	ah-ven-eer	An **ad**v**en**t calendar focuses on what is to come, in the future	Future	

Word or phrase	Pronunciation guide	Aide-mémoire	English meaning	Check
Projets (mpl) d'avenir	praw-zhay dah-ven-eer	Projects for the time to come (avenir). The advent (the coming) the future.	Future plans	
Impression (f)	ahm-press-yaw		Impression	
Interview (f)	ahn-tair-view		Interview	
Emploi (m)	amw-pl-wah	**Emplo**yment	Job	
Offre (f) d'emploi	off-reuh dawm-pl-wah	**Off**er of **emplo**yment	Job offer	
Lettre (f)	let-reuh		Letter	
Propriétaire (m/f)	prop-ree-ay-tair	**Propriet**or is English for owner	Owner	
Lettre (f) de motivation	let-reuh deuh moh-tee-vass-yaw	Letter about what motivates you	Personal statement	
Poste (m)	pawst	A post is a position in a company	Position	
Magasin (m)	mag-ah-zah	This shop sells magazines and many other things. Fish**mon**g**er**, **mag**asin.	Shop	
Conditions (fpl) d'emploi	kawn-deese-yaw dawm-pl-wah	Conditions of employment are terms of employment	Terms of employment	
Centre (m) de formation	sawn-treuh deuh for-mass-yaw	Forming someone is shaping someone, or training	Training centre	
Varié(e/s)	vah-ree-ay		Varied	
Bien payé(e/s)/ rémunéré(e/s)	bee-yeh pay-yay/ ray-moo-nay-ray	Payé is quite similar. Remuneration means payment.	Well-paid	
Travail (m)	trah-vye	Travails are hardships that must be undergone, like work	Work	
Stage (m)	stah-zheuh	You go through **stage**s on the road to improvement, gaining experience at each **stag**e	Work experience/ placement	
Faire un stage	fair ahn stah-zheuh	Faire, **fare**well (means do well). You go through **stage**s on the road to improvement.	Work placement, to do a	

Practise!

Translate the following into French:

1. I wanted to work in a shop which is close to my house because it is a job that is well-paid and varied.

_____

_____

2. I made an application for to be (a) cashier in a supermarket.

_____

_____

3. I went to the training centre and I learned how *(apprendre à)* to write *(écrire)* a personal statement.

_____

_____

4. The owner of the shop was impressed *(impressionné(e))* by my attitude.

_____

_____

5. I did a course for to learn how to work in a shop.
[Note: The odd phrasing of the English reflects how it would be said in French]

_____

_____

6. The careers advisor told me to think about my future. *(told me to think about my future – m'a dit de penser à mon avenir.)*

_____

_____

7. Advertising is important for business.

_____

_____

8. I have big *(big – de grandes)* ambitions and I don't want a job which is badly paid.

_____

_____

9. I received the job offer after having done the interview. *(reçu – past part of recevoir, to receive; après avoir fait – after having done.)*

_____

_____

10. My dream is to receive a job offer from West Ham United.

_____

_____

6: La gestion de l'argent
[Money management]

Word or phrase	Pronunciation guide	Aide-mémoire	English meaning	Check
Publicité (f)	poo-blee-see-tay	There is no such thing as bad **publicit**y. Publicity is advertising.	Advertising	
Conseil (m)	kaw-say	Counsel is advice	Advice	
Banque (f)	bawnk		Bank	
Carte (f) bancaire	kaahrt bawn-kair	Banker card	Bank card	
Billet (m) de banque	bee-yay deuh bawnk	A bill is a note, a dollar bill for example	Banknote	
Billet	bee-yay	A dollar bill	Bill	
Espèces (fpl)	ess-pess	In es**pieces**. Pieces of cash as opposed to a cheque.	Cash	
Argent (m) liquide	aahr-zhaw lee-keed	Liquid silver (argento, Ag) as opposed to a solid cheque.	Cash	
Bon marché	baw maahr-shay	Good markets (bon marché – good market) have cheaply-priced products	Cheap	
Choix (m)	shwah		Choice	
Pièce (f)	pee-yess	'Pieces of eight' were silver coins. A silver piece is a silver coin.	Coin	
Consultation (f)	kaw-soohl-tass-yaw		Consultation	
Guichet (m)	gee-shay	Money comes **gush**ing out the guichet	Counter (bank, train station)	
Comptoir (m)	kawn-twaahr	-oir often changes a verb into a noun. Compter – counter.	Counter (shop)	
Carte (f) de crédit	kaahrt deuh kray-dee		Credit card	
Carte (f) de retrait	kaahrt deuh euh-tray	Retrait – retreat, draw back, take out, debit from your account	Debit card	
Grand magasin (m)	graw mag-ah-zah	Big shop is a department store	Department store	
Euro (m)	euh-roh		Euro	
Taux (m) de change	toh deuh shaw-zheuh	A **ta**lly is a measurement, it indicates 'rate' like the **ta**ux	Exchange rate	
Cher(s)/chère(s)	shair	If someone is dear to you, they are **cher**ished	Expensive	
Cadeau (m)	kah-doh	What is in the caddie's bag? A gift for the golfer.	Gift	
Assurance (f)	ah-soo-rawss		Insurance	
Emploi (m)	awm-plwah	**Emplo**yment	Job	
Boulot (m)	bouh-loh	'Métro Boulot Dodo' describes the Parisian rat-race: train, work, sleep	Work	
Monnaie (f)	maw-nay	Link with **mone**y. Just remember that this is a false friend for a change!	Loose change	

Word or phrase	Pronunciation guide	Aide-mémoire	English meaning	Check
Bosser (v)	baw-say	If you don't work hard your **boss** will work you over!	Work (slang)	
Argent (m)	ahr-zhaw	Argento, a shop that sells silver. Ag, chemical symbol for silver. Silver coins, money.	Money	
Loterie nationale (f)	loh-tay-ree nass-yawn-al		National lottery	
En promotion	awe proh-moh-see-yaw	Shops **promot**e special offers so that we are aware of them	On offer	
Petit job (m)	peuh-tee job	Petit (small) because it is not a career. It is a part-time job.	Part-time job	
Argent (m) de poche	ahr-zhaw deuh posh	Poche – pouch, pocket. Ag (Argento, a silver shop). Pocket silver (money).	Pocket money	
Poste (f)	pawst	Note that le (m) post means 'post' (as in a job)	Post office	
Livre (f) sterling	lee-vreuh stair	**lb** (abbreviation of **libra**), is the old symbol for a pound, weight, link to **livre**	Pound sterling	
Cadeau (m)	kah-doh	What is the **cadd**ie carrying in that bag? Is it a present for the golfer?	Present	
Prix (m)	pree	Grand Prix. A grand prix means a big prize or a big price.	Price/prize	
Porte-monnaie (m)	port-maw-nay	Porters carry luggage. Here we have a little carrier for change, a purse.	Purse	
Tarif (m)	tah-reef	A tariff is a price	Rate, price list	
Ticket (m) de caisse	tee-kay deuh kess	A ticket from the **cash**ier. La caisse – the till, where the cash is.	Receipt	
Reçu (m)	reuh-soo	**Reç**u means received. What is received as proof of payment.	Receipt	
Risque (m)	reesk		Risk	
Les soldes (fpl)	lay sawld	**So**l**des** ressembles sales. Things that are **sold** cheaply.	Sales	
Magasin (m)	mah-gah-zah	Monger, like fish**mong**er, iron**mong**er, linked to **ma**g**asin**, shop	Shop	
Centre (m) commercial	sawn-treuh caw-mair-see-ahl	Commercial centre, shopping centre	Shopping centre	
Offre (f) spéciale	off-reuh spay-see-ahl		Special offer	
Pourboire (m)	pore-bwahr	Pour boire, **for b**eve**r**age. A tip, given to a waiter so he can buy a drink.	Tip	
Travail (m) bénévole	trah-vye bay-nay-vawl	Benevolance – kindness with nothing in return, voluntary. Travails – toil, ordeal, work.	Voluntary work	
Portefeuille (m)	pore-teuh fay-yeuh	A portfolio, a big wallet carrying paintings. From carry (porter) leaf of paper (feuille).	Wallet	

Practise!

Complete the following sentences with the correct word from the word list:

1. La machine à café que j'ai achetée était cassée donc j'ai dû l'échanger contre une nouvelle en présentant mon:

_____

2. On peut acheter les vêtements moins chers si on les achète dans les:

_____

3. Si on investit sur la bourse (the stock market), on prend un:

_____

4. Un jour j'aimerais beaucoup gagner le gros lot dans la:

_____

5. C'était l'anniversaire de mon frère donc j'ai utilisé tout mon argent de poche pour lui acheter un:

_____

6. Quand on paie un repas au restaurant, c'est sympa de donner au serveur un:

_____

7. J'ai acheté trois paquets de Hobnobs (des biscuits) car ils étaient en:

_____

8. "I'm loving it": C'est pour un restaurant de fast-food. C'est une:

_____

9. Quand j'ai voulu payer, j'ai compris, à mon horreur, que j'avais perdu mon:

_____

10. Il y a beaucoup de produits différents à acheter dans un:

_____

7. Les projets et les métiers
[Future plans and professions]

Word or phrase	Pronunciation guide	Aide-mémoire	English meaning	Check
Acteur/actrice (m/f)	ak-teuhr/ak-treece		Actor/actress	
Hôtesse (f) de l'air	oh-tess deuh lair		Air hostess	
Steward (m)	stew-aahrd		Air steward	
Apprenti/ apprentie (m/f)	ah-prawn-tee	The French verb, 'to learn' is apprendre – what an apprentice does	Apprentice	
Apprentissage (m)	ah-prawn-tee sah-zheuh		Apprenticeship	
Architecte (m/f)	arsh-ee-tekt		Architect	
Artiste (m/f)	ar-teest		Artist	
Chez moi	shay mwah	Chez moi (at my place) chez toi (at your place), chez lui (at his place), chez elle etc	At home	
Chez McDo	shay mac-doh	McDo – McDonald's	At McDonalds	
À la maison	ah lah may-zaw	Maison linked to **ma**n**s**i**o**n, big house	At my house	
À notre maison/ chez nous	ah nawt-treuh may-zaw/shay nouh	**N**o**tr**e – **o**u**r**. Cathédrale de Notre Dame de Paris, Cathedral of **our** Lady of Paris.	At our house	
Chez le dentiste	shay leuh dawn-teest	At the dentist. Chez l'opthalmogue – at the optician, chez le vétérinaire etc.	At the dentist	
Boulanger/ boulangère (m/f)	bouh-law-zhay/ bouh-law-zhair	**Boul**e de pâte, a **ball** of dough – for making bread	Baker	
Employé(e) de banque (m/f)	awm-plwy-yeah deuh bawnk	Employee of bank	Bank employee	
Maçon(ne) (m/f)	mah-saw	A mason is a person who works with stone	Builder	
Chauffeur/ chauffeuse de bus (m/f)	show-feuhr/ show-feuze deuh boose	Chauffeur is the English word for a paid driver	Bus driver	
Ennui (m)	awe-nwee	Being bored is **ennui**-ing (annoying)	Boredom	
Chef (m)/chef (f)	sheff	Chief, boss	Boss	
Patron/patronne (m/f)	pah-traw/ pah-trawn	Boss saint of Ireland, patron saint, Patrick. Prince Charles, patron of the Duke of Edinburgh Award Scheme.	Boss	
Homme (m) d'affaires	awm dah-fair	**Hom**o sapiens – man. D'affaire – affairs, business affairs.	Business man	
Femme (f) d'affaires	fam dah-fair	Femme – **fem**ale, woman. d'affaires – affairs, business affairs.	Business woman	
Boucher/ bouchère (m/f)	bouh-shay/ bouh-shair	Bouche – mouth. A butcher, (boucher) provides items for the mouth.	Butcher	
Certificat (m)	sair-tee-fee-kah		Certificate	
Fonctionnaire (m/f)	fonks-yawn-air	Carries out a function for society	Civil servant	
Curé (m)	coo-ray	A **cur**ate is a preacher in the Ch. of Ireland	Clergyman	

Word or phrase	Pronunciation guide	Aide-mémoire	English meaning	Check		
Informaticien/ ...cienne (m/f)	ah-for-mah-tee-see-yeah ...see-yen	IT means Information Technology	Computer technician			
Informatique (f)	ah-for-mah-teek	IT means Information Technology which is a synonym for computing	Computing			
Licence (f)	lee-sawss	A licence, a piece of paper proving you are capable of something, like a degree	Degree (bachelor's)			
Dentiste (m/f)	daw-teest		Dentist			
Diplôme (m)	dee-plome	A diploma is a qualification	Diploma qualification			
Médecin (m/f)	made-sah	Prescribes medicine	Doctor			
Electricien/ electricienne (m/f)	ay-lek-tree-see-yeah, ...-see-yenn		Electrician			
Employé(e)	awm-plwy-yay		Employee			
Ingénieur(e)	ah-zhay-nee-yeuhr	Ingénieur is pretty similar to engineer	Engineer			
Enthousiasme (m)	awn-touh-zee-az-meuh		Enthusiasm			
Explication (f)	eks-plee-kass-yaw	Explication and explanation are very similar	Explanation			
Usine (f)	oo-zeen	Factories are oozing (**usine**) a lot of energy	Factory			
Fac (f)	fak	The Faculty of Medicine is the Medicine department at a University	Faculty, slang for Uni			
Fermier/ fermière (m/f)	fair-mee-yay/ fair-mee-yair	**Fermier** and farmer	Farmer			
Pompier/ pompière (m/f)	pawm-pee-yeah/ pawm-pee-yair	A person who uses the pump (for water)	Firefighter			
Membre (m) de l'équipage	mawm-breuh deuh lay-keep-ah-zheuh	The équipage is the crew, they are the essential equipment on the flight	Flight attendant			
Courant(e)	kouh-raw/ kouh-rawnt	Courant – running, flowing (like a courier). That is how you speak, fluently.	Fluent			
Couramment	kouh-rah-maw	Adding -ment is how you make an adverb in French, e.g. patient > patiement. Coura-mment really means 'runningly'. 'Fluidly'.	Fluently			
Jardinier/ jardinière (m/f)	zhar-dee-nee-yeah, ...-nee-yair	J**arde**n	Gardener			
Doué(s)/doué(es)	douh-ay	Donate is to give. A donor gives. é is the equivalent of -ed. Gifted.	Gifted			
Épicier/épicière (m/f)	ay-pee-see-ay/ ay-pee-see-yair	é at the start of the word replaces an s. Grocers were originally spice merchants.	Grocer			
Coiffeur/coiffeuse (m/f)	kwaff-euhr, kwaff-euhze	A quiff is created or cut by the hairdresser	Hairdresser			
Dans une banque (f)	dawz-oon-bawnk	Da**n**s means **in**	In a bank			
Dans un cabinet (m) médical	dawz-ah-kah-bee-nay may-dee-kahl	Imagine you are a tiny elf in a medical cabinet. Like a doctor's surgery.	In a doctor's surgery			
Dans un garage (m)	dawz-ah gah-rah-zheuh	Da**n**s means **in**	In a garage			

Word or phrase	Pronunciation guide	Aide-mémoire	English meaning	Check
Dans un hôpital (m)	dawz-ahn oh-pee-tahl	Da**n**s means i**n**. ô denotes s after the o.	In a hospital	
Dans un bureau (m)	dawz-ahn booh-roh	A bureau is an office. A bureau de change is an office where money is exchanged.	In an office	
Dans un parc (m)	dawz-ahn paark		In a park	
Connaissance (f)	koh-ness-awss	Cognescence is awareness, knowledge. A reconnaissance trip is to gain knowledge.	Knowledge	
Avocat/avocate (m/f)	ah-voh-kah/ ah-voh-kat	An **ad**v**ocat**e for a client is someone who speaks for a client, like a lawyer.	Lawyer/solicitor	
Apprentissage (m)	ah-praw-teese-ah-zheuh	Apprendre – French verb, to learn. -age creates noun, e.g. garer, to park > garage.	Learning	
Conférence (f)	kaw-fay-rawss		Lecture/ conference	
Chauffeur/feuse de camion (m/f)	shoh-feur/...feuhz deuh cam-ee-yaw	Camion – 'Come ye on' board my lorry! **Chau**ffeurs warmed the car before driving.	Lorry driver	
Mécanicien/ mécanicienne (m/f)	may-can-eese-yeah/ ....-neese-yenn		Mechanic	
Entre deux âges (mpl)	awn-treuh deuhz-ah-zheuh	Entre, linked to inter which means between. Between two ages (old and young).	Middle-age	
D'âge (m) mûr	dah-zheuh moohr	Mûr is mature, demure	Middle-age	
Musicien(ne) (m/f)	mooh-zeese-yeah, mooh-zeese-yenn		Musician	
Ma carrière (f)	mah kaar-ee-yair	Carrière and career are pretty similar	My career	
Mon rêve (m)	maw rev	Revery is dreaminess. I dream that my car has lots of revs!	My dream	
Infirmier(ère) (m/f)	ah-fearm-yeah, ah-fearm-yair	Infirmary is a hospital, invalid	Nurse	
Troisième âge (m)	trwah-zee-em ah-zheuh	Troisième means 3rd. The third age, not young (age 1), not middle-aged (age 2).	Old age	
Dehors (m)	deuh-oar	Hors means 'out of'. Hors service – out of order. De means of. So, de hors – of out of.	Outside	
Surchargé(e/s)	soohr-shar-zhay	Sur – on/over. Charged means loaded, linked to cargo. 'Charge your glass!'	Overworked/ overloaded	
Peintre (m/f)	pan-treuh	Similar to painter	Painter/ decorator	
Lieu (m) de travail	lee-yeuh deuh trav-eye	In lieu of – in stead/place of. Time off 'in lieu'. Tenant holds a place. Lieutenant.	Place of work	
Plombier/ plombière (m/f)	plawm-bee-yeah/ plawm-bee-yair	Plumbum is Latin for 'lead'– pipes used to be made of lead, chemical symbol Pb	Plumber	
Policier/ policière (m/f)	poh-lease-yeah/ poh-lease-yair		Police officer	
Facteur/ factrice (m/f)	fac-teur/ fac-treese	A 'facture' is a bill and the 'facteur' delivers them. Sorry! He delivers the 'facts'.	Postman/ woman	
Instituteur/ institutrice (m/f)	ah-stee-toot-euhr/ ah-stee-toot-reese	Initiates the teaching	Primary teacher	

Word or phrase	Pronunciation guide	Aide-mémoire	English meaning	Check
Métier (m)	may-tee-ay	Jack of all trades and **ma**s**ter** of none! **Ma**s**ter** builder = professional builder.	Profession	
Profession (f)	pro-fess-yaw		Profession	
Programmeur (euse) (m/f)	pro-grah-meuhr, pro-gram-euhze		Programmer	
Incivilités (fpl)	ah-see-vee-lee-tay	If you are not being civil, incivil (uncivil), you are being rude	Rudeness	
Salaire (m)	sah-lair		Salary	
Vendeur(euse) (m/f)	vawn-deuhr, vawn-deuhze	Vending machine, vendor	Sales assistant	
Représentant(e) (m/f)	rep-ray-zawn-taw, ...-tawnt	A sales **rep rep**resents the company	Salesman/woman	
École (f)	ay-kawl	É at the start of a word replaces an 's'	School	
Professeur (m/f)	prof	Professeur – a higher level teacher, not primary	Secondary teacher	
Secrétaire (m/f)	seuh-kray-tair		Secretary	
Á son propre compte	ah saw prop-reuh cawnt	On my proper account	Self-employed	
Marchand(e) (m/f)	marsh-aw, ...awnd	Merchant, market	Shopkeeper	
Magasin (m)	mah-gah-zah	Monger, fish**mong**er, iron**mong**er, linked to **mag**as**in**, shop. Magasin sells magazines.	Shop	
Soldat (m/f)	soll-dah	**Sold**at	Soldier	
Chirurgien(ne) (m/f)	she-ruur-zhee-yeah, ...-yenn	Chir**urgi**en	Surgeon	
Tâche (f)	tash	Task and tâche are pretty similar	Task	
Enseignant (e) (m/f)	awn-sen-yaw, awn-sen-yawnt	'E' for education	Teacher (general word)	
Technicien/technicienne (m/f)	tek-nee-see-yeah/...see-yenn		Technician	
Thème (m)	tem		Theme	
Confiance (f)	kaw-fee-oss	**Confi**ance is confidence, is trust	Trust/confidence	
Serveur(euse)	sair-veuhr, sair-veuhze	Serves meals, drinks, drunks	Waiter/waitress	
Bien/mal équipé(e/s)	bee-yeah/ mahl ay-keep-ay	Bien – well – **ben**efit, **ben**efactor. Mal – badly – **mal**icious, **mal**nourished. é = ed.	Well/badly equipped	
Boulot (m)	bouh-loh	'Métro Boulot Dodo' describes the Parisian rat-race: train, **work**, sleep	Work (slang)	
Ouvrier(ère) (m/f)	ouh-vree-yeah, ouh-vree-yair	A few similar letters (w)**o**uv**ri**er, just need a 'k'.	Worker	
Atelier (m)	Ah-tell-ee-ay	If you have no room inside your house for a workshop, put it in the **att**ic.	Workshop	
Souci (m)	Souh-see	Sans souci is an expression used in English. No worries if you can't remember!	Worry	

Practise!

Assortissez les métiers aux descriptions ci-dessous. *(Match the jobs to the descriptions below.)*

1. On sert dans un restaurant: _____

2. On enseigne dans une école: _____

3. On vend: _____

4. On répare les voitures: _____

5. On représente en justice: _____

6. On prêche: _____

7. On conduit un bus: _____

8. On vend les saucisses: _____

9. On peint: _____

8. Adjectifs communs
(Common adjectives)

Word or phrase	Pronunciation guide	Aide-mémoire	English meaning	Check
Étonné(e)/s	ay-tonnay	'é' replaces 's' at start of the word. é at the end is 'ed', e.g. 'stoned'. Like astonished.	Amazed, astonished	
Pénible(s)	pain-ee-bleuh	If it is annoying, it is **pain**ful. If it's painful it's annoying.	Annoying	
Embêtant(e/s)	awm-bet-awe/ awm-bet-awnt	-ant at the end is -ing. ê denotes 's' after 'e'. Bête – beast – raging, enraging, annoying.	Annoying	
Casse-pieds	kass-pee-yay	Casser – to break, to **cra**ck. Pied, pedestrian, foot. Literally, foot-breaking, which is clearly annoying.	Annoying	
Soucieux(se)	souh-see-yeuh (yeuze)	Under (**sou**s, like sub) the weight of the world, skies (ceiling, ciel, **cieux**).	Anxious/ worried	
Affreux/ affreuse(s)	aff-reuh/ aff-reuhze	Affreux and **a**w**f**ul are quite similar	Awful	
Mauvais(e/s)	moh-vay/ moh-vays	**Ma**(l) tells us of badness. **Ma**licious, **ma**laria, **ma**lnutrition. Vais – going. Bad going bad.	Bad	
Ennuyeux/ ennuyeuse(s)	awn-wee-yeuh/ awn-wee-yeuhze	**Enn**uy**e**ux is quite close to **ann**o**yi**ng. Rememember that '-eux' is an adjective.	Boring/ annoying	
Compliqué(e/s)	kawm-plee-kay		Complicated	
Cool	couhl		Cool	
Mignon(s)/ mignonne(s)	mean-yaw/ mean-yawn	**Min**nie Mouse is so cute but when she is tired, she can do a 'mean yawn'!	Cute	
Cher(s)/chère(s)	shair	If someone is **cher**ished, they are held dear	Dear	
Ravi(e/s)	rah-vee	If you look **ravi**shing, you look delightful. You feel delighted if you are told you are **ravi**shing.	Delighted	
Difficile(s)	dee-fee-seel	**Diffic**ul**t**	Difficult	
Dégoutant(e/s)	day-gouh-taw/ day-gouh-tawnt	Linked to **dis**g**u**s**tin**g	Disgusting	
Nul(s)/nulle(s)	noohl	Nil is zero which is not good, dreadful. This is a general word meaning not good.	Dreadful	
Rêveur/rêveuse	rev-eurr/rev-euze	Lost in reverie is to be lost in dreams. Trevor the reveur, Trevor the dreamer.	Dreamy	
Facile(s)	fah-seel	Facile – easy, the opposite of di-facile, like fuse and de-fuse	Easy	
Amusant(e/s)	ah-moo-zaw	Amusing	Entertaining, funny	
Passionnant(e/s)	pass-yawn-aw/nt	Passion and excitement are linked. -ant at the end of a word denotes an adjective.	Exciting	
Peureux/ pereuse	peuh-reuh/ peuh-reuze	**Pe**trified, scared	Fearful	
Drôle(s)	drole	Drôle is used in English to mean funny, in a dry sort of way. Drooling with laughter.	Funny, amusing	

Word or phrase	Pronunciation guide	Aide-mémoire	English meaning	Check
Marrant(e)/s	mah-raw/ mah-rawnt	**Marr**ant links to **merr**y. **Merr**imen**t** and fun are linked.	Funny	
Rigolo(s)/ rigolote(s)	ree-goh-loh/ ree-goh-lot	**Rig**ol**o** reminds us of giggle. When you giggle you have found something funny.	Funny	
Bon(s)/bonne(s)	baw/bawn		Good	
Formidable(s)	for-mee-dah-bleuh	If something is formidable it is great	Great	
Génial(e)s/ géniaux	zhay-nee-al/ zhay-nee-oh	A great idea is a **geni**us idea	Great	
Chouette(s)	schwett	It just sounds great. Sweaty (schwett, see pronunciation) is slang for great.	Great (positive)	
Content(e/s)	kawn-taw (-tawnt)	Content is happy	Happy	
J'ai envie d'y aller	zhay aw-vee dee al-ay	J'ai = I have. **Env**y (desire) to go (go down an **alle**y). Y = there. 'Allons-y' = 'Let's go there'.	I'm excited about going	
Pressé(e/s)	press-ay	**Press**ed upon to do something, **press**urised, **press**-ganged, you are in a hurry.	In a hurry	
Incroyable(s)	ahn-krwy-ah-bleuh	**Incr**edi**ble** is close to **incr**oya**ble**	Incredible	
Intelligent(e/s)	ahn-tel-ee-zhaw/ ahn-tel-ee-zhawnt		Intelligent	
Intéressant(e/s)	ahn-tay-res-saw	Interesting (note, no '**t**' in French before the 'ant' which means 'ing') Intéress ant.	Interesting	
Ça te décontracte	sah teuh day-con-tract	Contracted, tight, tense. De-contracted, not tight, not tense.	It relaxes you	
Gentil(s)/ gentille(s)	zhawn-tee/ zhawn-tee-yeuh	**Gentl**e is linked to kind	Kind	
Paresseux/ paresseuse(s)	pah-ress-euh/ pah-ress-euze	A **paras**ite sucks someone else's blood, can't be bothered making its own	Lazy	
Merveilleux/ merveilleuse(s)	mair-vay-yeuh/ mair-vay-yeuhze	Merveilleux and marvellous are closely linked	Marvellous	
Nouveau(x)/ nouvelle(s)	nouh-voh / nouh-vell	**Ne**w and **n**ouv**e**au are linked. A novel idea is a new idea. A novice is new to something.	New	
Neuf(s)/ neuve(s)	neuhff/neuhve	**Ne**uf and and **ne**w, closely linked ·	New (brand new)	
Bruyant(e/s)	brwee-yaw (-yawnt)	Associated words: bustle, boisterous, battle, brute, bad, behaviour	Noisy	
Parfait(e/s)	par-fay/par-fet	Perfect and parfait are linked	Perfect	
Pratique(s)	prat-eek	Practical and pratique are linked	Practical	
Rasant(e/s)	rah-zaw	Rasant, linked to razor, shaving: not interesting at all.	Really boring	
Ridicule(s)	ree-dee-koohl		Ridiculous	
Sensas	senn-sass		Sensational	
Sérieux/ sérieuse(s)	say-ree-euh/ say-ree-euhze		Serious	

Word or phrase	Pronunciation guide	Aide-mémoire	English meaning	Check
Sportif(s)/ sportive(s)	spore-teef (teeve)		Sporty	
Bizarre(s)	bee-zaahr	Bizarre is strange	Strange	
Stressant(e/s)	stress-saw	Stressful, stressing	Stressful	
Strict(e/s)	streekt		Strict	
Fort(e/s)	fore (fort)	Strong like a **fort**ress, **Fort** Knox, **for**midable, **fort**itude	Strong	
Formidable	fore-mee-dah-bleuh	Formidable	Strongly impressive	
Moche(s)	mosh	Onamatopoeia is helpful here. How beautiful is mush? Not very! Pretty ugly actually.	Ugly	
Laid(e/s)	lay/led	Beautiful metal: gold, platinum, silver, bronze. Ugly metal: lead. Lead rhymes with dead.	Ugly	
Déplaisant(e/s)	day-plez-awe/ day-plez-awnt	Dé at the start of a word reverses the meaning of the rest of the word. Pleasant, unpleasant.	Unpleasant	
Utile(s)	ooh-teel	Utilise means use. Useful and utility are linked. A utility player is a useful player.	Useful	
Inutile(s)	een-ooh-teel	Un-useful. 'In' at the start of the word reverses the meaning of the rest of the word.	Useless	
On s'entend bien	awe sawn-taw byeah	An **enten**te is an agreement when both sides hear what the other is saying	We get on well	
Faible(s)	feb-leuh	Faible linked to feeble, weak	Weak	
Sage(s)	sah-zheuh	A wise old sage is well-behaved. Les dents de sagesse are wisdom teeth.	Well-behaved	
Connu(e/s)	con-ooh	Conscious, people are **con**scious of your existence	Well-known	
Inquiet/ inquiète	ah-kee-yay (-yet)	Sounds like anxious, if you are quiet, you are at ease, unquiet, anxious	Worried/ anxious	

Practise!

Comment est-ce que tu veux être décrit? (*How do you want to be described?*)
Put the most positive adjective first.

1. _____   2. _____

3. _____   4. _____

5. _____   6. _____

7. _____   8. _____

9: Comparatifs
[Comparatives]

Word or phrase	Pronunciation guide	Aide-mémoire	English meaning	Check
Beaucoup (de)	boh-kouh (deuh)	A coup de something, an amount of something. Beau coup, a nice (beautiful) amount of.	A lot (of)	
Aussi ... que	oh-see keuh	**Au**ss**i** ....is linked. **As** big **as**: **Au**ss**i** grand que (que can mean as).	As ... as	
Mauvais	moh-vay	**Ma** is the prefix (bit at the start of a word) that suggests bad, malicious, malpractice	Bad	
Mal	maahl	**Mal**practice, **mal**icious, badly	Badly	
Meilleur	may-yeuhr	A**melior**ate is an English word which means 'improve'. It is linked to meilleur.	Better (adj)	
Mieux	myeuh	A**melior**ate is an English word which means 'improve'. It is linked to mieux.	Better (adv)	
Peu de	peuh deuh	**P**eu is linked to **p**altry, **p**oor. These point to a small amount.	Few	
Moins de	mwah deuh	Moins links to minus, meaning less, subtracting, less. Less of is fewer.	Fewer	
Bon	baw	**Bon**-jour means good-day	Good (adj)	
Moins	mwah	Moins links to minus, meaning less, subtracting, less	Less	
Moins que	mwah keuh	Moins links to minus, meaning less, subtracting, less than	Less ... than	
Plus	plooh	Plus que. Plus is about more.	More	
Plus que	ploose keuh	Plus que – more than	More ... than	
Le mieux	leuh myeuh	A**melior**ate is an English word which means 'improve'. It is linked to mieux.	The best (adv)	
Le meilleur	leuh may-yeuhr	A**melior**ate is an English word which means 'improve'. It is linked to meilleur.	The best	
La meilleure	lah may-yeuhr	A**melior**ate is an English word which means 'improve'. It is linked to meilleur.	The best	
Les meilleur(e)s	lay may-yeuhr	A**melior**ate is an English word which means 'improve'. It is linked to meilleur.	The best	
Le moins	leuh mwah	Moins, minus, less. The less. The least.	The least	
La moins	lah mwah	Moins, minus, less. The less. The least.	The least	
Les moins	lay mwah	Moins, minus, less. The less. The least.	The least	
Le pire	leuh peer	Pierre est un pirate qui est pire que Paul. A poor pirate is worse than a good one.	The worst	
La pire	lah peer	Pierre est un pirate qui est pire que Paul. A poor pirate is worse than a good one.	The worst	
Les pires	lay peer	Pierre est un pirate qui est pire que Paul. A poor pirate is worse than a good one.	The worst (pl)	

Word or phrase	Pronunciation guide	Aide-mémoire	English meaning	Check
Le plus mal	leuh plooh mahl	**Mal**practice, **mal**icious, bad. Le plus mal. The more bad. The most bad, the worst.	The worst (adv)	
Bien	bee-yeah	**Ben**eficial, **ben**efactor, **ben**evolent. All to do with good or well. C'est bien, West Ham!	Well (adj)	
Bien	bee-yeah	**Ben**evolent means you do well for others. A **ben**efactor does well for others. West Ham joue bien.	Well (adv)	
Pire	peer	Pierre est un pirate qui est pire que Paul. A poor pirate is worse than a good one.	Worse (adj)	
Plus mal	plooh mahl	Plus – more. Mal is to with bad. **Mal**nourished, **mal**icious. More bad – worse.	Worse (adv)	

Practise!

Translate:

1. Elle est aussi intelligente que sa soeur mais sa soeur est meilleure en sport:

_____

_____

2. Il écrit plus mal que son frère et il est pire que son frère en maths:

_____

_____

3. J'ai moins d'argent dans ma poche mais un peu d'argent sur mon compte:

_____

_____

4. Ils sont bons en physique mais mauvais en chimie:

_____

_____

5. Elle est la meilleure de tous les élèves:

_____

_____

6. Il est le moins intéressé de tous les étudiants:

_____

_____

7. Ils sont les pires élèves de toute l'histoire:

_____

_____

8. C'est un bon garçon qui travaille bien: (note, in this phrase, 'c'est' is translated as 'he is', not 'it is')

_____

_____

10: Les jours de la semaine, les mois et les saisons
(Days of the week, months and seasons)

Word or phrase	Pronunciation guide	Aide-mémoire	English meaning	Check
Jour (m)	jouhr	A **jour**nal is written every day. Bon-jour means good-day.	Day	
Semaine (f)	seuh-men	**Se**ven days in one of these	Week	
Lundi (m)	laan-dee	Lune – moon. Di – like day. Moon-day.	Monday	
Mardi (m)	maar-dee	Lundi (L) is followed by Mardi (M). L M, alphabetically next. It must be Tuesday.	Tuesday	
Mercredi (m)	mair-kred-ee	Market-day (Mercredi) is often Wednesday. Or 'middleday'.	Wednesday	
Jeudi (m)	zheuh-dee	Jupiter and Thor are both gods of thunder	Thursday	
Vendredi (m)	vawn-dred-ee	V...redi – V...riday	Friday	
Samedi (m)	sam-dee	**Sa**turday	Saturday	
Dimanche (m)	dee-maw-sheuh	One day of rest, one day ends differently (i.e. not in 'di')	Sunday	

Word or phrase	Pronunciation guide	Aide-mémoire	English meaning	Check
Mois (m)	leuh mwah	**Mo**nth	Month	
L'année (f)	lannay	**Ann**ual is every year	Year	
En janvier	awe jaw-vee-ay		**In** January	
Janvier	jaw-vee-ay		January	
Février	fay-vree-ay		February	
Mars	maarss		March	
Avril	ah-vreel		April	
Mai	may		May	
Juin	jwaah		June	
Juillet	jwee-yay	**Jui**llet, like July	July	
Août	ouht	^ tells you next letter is 's', as in Augu**st**	August	
Septembre	sep-tawm-breuh		September	
Octobre	oc-tawb-reuh		October	
Novembre	noh-vawm-breuh		November	
Décembre	day-sawm-breuh		December	

Word or phrase	Pronunciation guide	Aide-mémoire	English meaning	Check
Saison (f)	say-zaw		Season	
Au **prin**temps (m)	oh-prahn-taw	Prim (rose) time (temps) – printemps – they grow first among flowers in spring.	Spring	
En été (m)	awn ay-tay	'Estival' means summery in French. Festival is a combination of this and party (fête).	Summer	
En automne (m)	awn oh-tawn		Autumn	
En hiver (m)	awn ee-vair	**Hi**ber**nate**	Winter	

11: Descriptions, surtout de couleur
[Descriptions, especially of colour]

Word or phrase	Pronunciation guide	Aide-mémoire	English meaning	Check
Noir(e/s)	nwaahr	'Nowhere' to be seen in the dark	Black	
Blond(s)/ blonde(s)	blaw/blawnd		Blond	
Bleu(e/s)	bleuh		Blue	
Marron	mah-raw	Maroon is a reddy-brown	Brown	
Brun(e/s)	brah, broon	Brown	Brown	
Châtain(s)/ châtaine(s)	shah-tah/ shah-ten	**Ch**est**nut**. The â denotes an 's'.	Chestnut brown	
Cercle (m)	sair-kleuh		Circle	
Couleur (f)	couh-leuhr		Colour	
Foncé(e/s)	faw-say	Your face darkens when you **frown**	Dark	
Sombre(s)	sawm-breuh	Sombre is dark, dull	Dull, dark	
En or	awn-ohr	El d**or**ado means the Golden One. Aur**or**a borealis – the Northern Lights.	Gold	
Vert(s)/verte(s)	vair, vairt	**Ver**dant means green	Green	
Gris/grise(s)	gree, greeze	Sounds like	Grey	
Noisette	nwah-zet	**N**u**t** and **n**oise**t**te	Hazel(nut) colour	
Clair(e/s)	klair	Clear and light	Light	
Long(s)/ longue(s)	long/lon-geuh		Long	
De taille moyenne	deuh tye mwy-enn	'Taille' linked to tailor, tailler, to cut. **M**edia**n** (**m**oye**n**ne) average. Of average cut.	Medium-sized	
Orange	oh-raw-zheuh		Orange	
Pâle(s)	pahl		Pale	
Rose(s)	rows	A rosey colour is pink	Pink	
Pourpre(s)	pouh-preuh		Purple	
Violet(s)/ violette(s)	vee-oh-lay/ vee-oh-lett		Purple (violet)	
Rouge(s)	rouh-zheuh	Ladies wear 'rouge' as a blusher	Red	
Roux(rousse/s)	rouh, rouhsse	Russet is gingery colour, rust colour	Red, ginger (hair)	
Rond(s)/ ronde(s)	raw/rawnd		Round	
Court(s)/ courte(s)	kouhr/kouhrtt	If you are **curt** with someone, you are **short** with them	Short	
En argent	awn ahr-zhaw	Argento is a shop that sells silver. Ag is the chemical symbol for silver.	Silver	

Word or phrase	Pronunciation guide	Aide-mémoire	English meaning	Check
Petit(s)/petite(s)	peuh-tee/ peuh-teet	**Petty** cash is **small** change. **Petite** is used to describe a small girl.	Small	
Carré (m)	kah-ray	Carré linked to **qua**d**r**ant	Square	
Grand(s)/ grande(s)	graw/grawnd	Un grand projet, a grand project, a tall order.	Tall	
Blanc(s)/ blanche(s)	blaw, blawwsh	Blank is white	White	
Jaune(s)	zhoan	Jaundice is a yellowing of the skin	Yellow	

Practise!

Translate the following descriptions:

1. J'ai les cheveux longs et les yeux bleus: _____

2. Elle est petite avec les cheveux courts: _____

3. Ma souris est blanche et noire: _____

4. Il est de taille moyenne, comme moi: _____

5. Les violets et les roses sont rouges: _____

6. Les cheveux noirs foncés sont cool: _____

12: Salutations
(Greetings)

Word or phrase	Pronunciation guide	Aide-mémoire	English meaning	Check
Félicitations	fay-lee-see-tass-yaw	**Felicit**y, a girl's name. It means happiness. Happiness**ations**.	Congratulations	
Bon appétit	bonn app-ay-tee	I wish you 'Good appetite' for your meal	Enjoy your meal	
Bonsoir	bonn swaahr	Good soirée (means good evening party)	Good evening	
Bonne nuit	bonn nwee	Good **n**octurnal, **n**igh**t**	Good night	
Bon voyage	baw veuh-wy ah-zheuh	Good voyage (trip)	Good trip	
Au revoir!	oh-rev-wire	Until the re-**vi**ew, re-see	Goodbye	
Bon anniversaire	bonn ann-ee-vair-sair	Good anniversary (of your birth)	Happy Birthday	
Bonne année	bonn ann-ay	Good **ann**ual greeting	Happy New Year	
Allô	ah-loh	Allo, allo – sounds like you are taking the Michael	Hello (on the phone)	
Bonjour	baw-jouhr	Bon – good, jour – day. Good Day = Hello.	Hello/good morning	
Coucou	kouh-kouh	What cuckoos say when they poke their heads out of a clock	Hey there (for someone you know)	
Au secours	oh seuh-kouhr	**Cours** – from running (a course), run to help. 'Succour' is an old English word for 'help'.	Help!	
Salut	sah-loo	I salute you	Hi/Bye-bye	
Comment vas-tu?	kaw-maw vah-too	Comment on how you are going	How are you?	
Comment ça va?	kaw-maw sah vah?	Comment on how it vavavoom, goes	How are you?	
Ça va?	sah-vah?	Vavavoom – go, it goes, I'm going well	How is it going?	
J'ai onze ans, et toi?	zhay awze awe, ay twah	Onze and eleven both start with vowels and involve n & e	I am 11 and you?	
Je m'appelle ... et toi?	zheuh mah-pel... ay twah	**Appeal** – call, I call me....Al	I am called ... And you?	
Je dois partir	zheuh dwah par-teer	Partir – de**part**, leave	I have to leave	
J'habite à Belfast, et vous?	zhah-beet ah belfast, ay vouh?	In**habit**	I live in Belfast, and you (formal)?	
Ça fait longtemps!	sah-fay long-taw	That **fa**bricates, (makes) **long t**ime	It's been a while	
Ça va bien merci et vous?	sah vah bee-yeah mair-see ay vouh	Vavavoom – go, bien – **ben**efit, good, well	It's going well thanks and you (pl)?	
Joyeux Noël	zheuh-wy euh noh ell	Joyous Noël (joy for Noël at Christmas)	Merry Christmas	

Word or phrase	Pronunciation guide	Aide-mémoire	English meaning	Check
Mon anniversaire est le quatre février	mon ... ay leuh cat fay-vree-ay	My anniversary, **quar**t**er** (four), February (very similar)	My birthday is the fourth of February	
Rien de special!	ree-yeah deuh spay-see-al	Nothing of **special**	Nothing much	
Bien sûr!	bee-yeah soohr	**Well sure**! – to be sure, to be sure, of course	Of course!	
D'accord	dah-kohr	We are of one **accord** – we agree, I agree with you, OK	OK, agreed	
S'il te plaît	seel-teuh-play	Si – if, if it to you (te) is **pl**e**a**s**i**ng	Please	
S'il vous plaît	seel-vouh-play	Si – if, if it to you (vous) is **pl**e**a**s**i**ng	Please (formal, plural)	
À plus tard/À plus	ah ploo-taar/ ah ploose	**Tard**y is late, to plus (more) late, later	See you later	
À tout à l'heure	ah touht ah leurr	**To**p of the **hour** is when I'll see you	See you later	
À la prochaine	ah lah pro-shen	In the **pro**ximity is the area **next** to you	See you next time	
À bientôt	ah bee-yen toe	Bien – **ben**efit – good, well. The 'ô' denotes an 's', so **tôt**, early **to**as**t**.	See you soon (well early)	
À demain	ah deuh-mah	Demain – de-marrah – tomorrow	See you tomorrow	
Désolé(e)	day-zoh-lay	I am feeling desolate, alone, no sole, sad, sorry	Sorry	
Merci	mair-see	Thank you for having **merc**y on me	Thanks	
Bienvenue	bee-yeah veuh-noo	Well, come (like you come to a venue)	Welcome	
Quel dommage!	kell doh-mah-zheuh	What (Which, kell the witch) a damage-ing, pitiful situation	What a pity!	
Quel âge as-tu?	kell ah-zheuh ah-too	Quel (Which, ke(i)ll the witch. Sorry Witch!) **age** **a**ve-yo**u**?	What (Which) age are you?	
Quoi de neuf?	kwah deuh neuhff	Quoi – what of **ne**w?	What's up?	
Comment est-ce que tu t'appelles?	kaw maw ess-keuh too tah-pel	**Appeal** – call, how is it that you **call** yourself?	What's your name?	
Où est-ce que tu habites?	ouh ess-keuh too ah-beet	Où – has one of the strokes of the 'w' of where sitting on its ù. Habites – In**habit** – live.	Where do you live?	
Quelle est la date de ton anniversaire?	kell-ay lah dat deuh tawn ...	Kell, which is the date of your anniversary?	Which is the date is your birthday?	

Practise!

Use the information in this section to create the following conversation in French:

1. A: Hello, how are you, and what's your name?

_____

B: Hello, my name is Peter and I am well, thank you. And you?

_____

2. A: I am called Bert. Which is the date is your birthday?

_____

B: My birthday is the 4th February and you?

_____

3. A: My birthday is the fifth of February. Where do you live?

_____

B: I live in Coleraine, and you?

_____

4. A: I live in Coleraine too. See you soon.

_____

B: Yes, until the next time.

_____

5. Make up another conversation below. This time with C & D, who know each other.

_____

_____

_____

_____

_____

_____

_____

_____

_____

_____

_____

_____

13: Les négations
(Negatives)

Word or phrase	Pronunciation guide	Aide-mémoire	English meaning	Check
Je **ne** fume **plus**	zheuh **neuh** foom **plooh**	No **plus** or extra smoking, no more, any more	**Any more** (e.g. I don't smoke any more)	
Je **ne** vois **ni** X **ni** Y	zheuh **neuh** vwah **nee** X **nee** Y	**N**either, **n**or, two 'n's like in English	**Neither** I see neither X nor Y	
Je **ne** mange **jamais**	zheuh **neuh** maw-zheuh **zhah-may**	Je **ne** mange **jamais** de la confiture – I never eat jam	**Never** I never eat	
Je **ne** vois **aucun** problème	zheuh **neuh** vwah **oh-kah** prob-lem	Aucun problème – no problem. Il **n**'y a **aucun** problème – There is no problem.	**No** I see no problem	
Je **ne** mange **pas**	zheuh **neuh** maw-zheuh **pah**	**Ne**... **pas**, **ne**gative. The shortest negative structure, like 'not' in English. 3 letters in 'not' and 'pas'.	**Not** I do not eat	
Je **ne** vois **personne**	zheuh **neuh** vwah **pair-sawn**	**Ne**gative. The **one** at the end of the word helps, i.e. no-one.	**Nobody** I see nobody/no-one	
Je **ne** mange **rien**	zheuh **neuh** maw-zheuh ree-yeah	**Ne**gative but nothing, '**de rien**' (of nothing) means 'it's nothing', 'don't mention it!'	**Nothing** I eat nothing	
Je **ne** vais **nulle** **part**	zheuh **neuh** vay **nool** **paarh**	**Ne**gative. Nul, **nil** as in zero, **part** of the world, going to **nil** part of the world.	**Nowhere** I'm going nowhere	
Je **ne** mange **que** les légumes	zheuh **neuh** maw-zheuh **keuh** lay lay-goom	Que toi means 'Only you'	**Only** I only eat vegetables	
Je **ne** travaille **pas** **encore**	zheuh **neuh** trav-eye **paz** **awn-kohr**	Pas encore. Not yet.	**Yet** I don't work yet	

Practise!

Translate the following sentences into English. Here are a few definitions, to help:

fumer	to smoke
faire	to do/make
pleurer	to cry
comprendre	to understand
gagner	to win
parler	to speak

1. Je ne fume pas.

_____

2. Il ne fait rien.

_____

3. Elle ne pleure jamais.

_____

4. Tu ne gagnes jamais.

_____

5. Nous ne comprenons personne.

_____

6. Il ne pleure plus.

_____

7. Je ne comprends aucune question.

_____

8. Il ne parle que l'anglais.

_____

9. Elle ne va nulle part.

_____

10. Il ne parle ni le français, ni l'allemand.

_____

14:

Les nombres et les numéros
[Cardinal numbers and ordinal numbers]

Word or phrase	Pronunciation guide	Aide-mémoire	English meaning	Check
Numéro	noo-may-roe	**Num**ber	Number	
Premier/ première	prem-ee-ay/ prem-ee-air	Premier league, first league. Prime Minister, first Minister.	First	
Fois (f)	fwah	**Fwahst** time la première fois – the first time	Time (occasion) (e.g. the first time)	
Dernier/ dernière	dair-nee-ay/ dair-nee-air	It rhymes with premier **but** is the exact opposite!	Last	
Deuxième	deuh-zee-em	Duo	Second	
Troisième	trwah-zee-em	Trio	Third	
Quatrième	kaat-ree-em	Quadrilateral, quad bike, quadrangle	Fourth	
Cinquième	sank-ee-em	Qu**in**tuplets (**Cinq**) – five babies	Fifth	
Sixième	see-zee-em		Six	
Vingt et unième	vahnt-ay oon-ee-em	Vant, tvent, twent, twenty	Twenty-first	
Un/une	ah/oon		1	
Deux	deuh	Duo	2	
Trois	trwah	Trio	3	
Quatre	cat-reuh	Quadrilateral, quad bike, quadrangle	4	
Cinq	sank	Qu**in**tuplets – five babies	5	
Six	seese		6	
Sept	set	September used to be the seventh month before July and August were added	7	
Huit	weet	They both end with a 't'	8	
Neuf	neuhff	Both start with 'n'	9	
Dix	deese	Decimal system – based on tens	10	
Onze	awnze	11 ounces	11	
Douze	douhze	A dozen is twelve	12	
Treize	trez	Trays carrying trios	13	
Quatorze	cat-oars	Quadrilateral, quad bike, quadrangle, cat-oars (miaow, row, row)	14	
Quinze	cans	Qu**in**tuplets – five babies	15	
Seize	says	'S' to start, like sixteen. Are you sixteen? Really? Who says (seize)?	16	
Dix-sept	deese-set		17	
Dix-huit	deese-weet		18	
Dix-neuf	deese-neuhff		19	
Vingt	vant	Vant, tvent, twent, twenty	20	

Word or phrase	Pronunciation guide	Aide-mémoire	English meaning	Check
Vingt-et-un	vant-ay-un		21	
Vingt-deux	vant-deuh		22	
Trente	trawnt	Link to trio	30	
Quarante	kah-rawnt	Quadrilateral, quad bike, quadrangle	40	
Cinquante	sank-awnt	Qu**in**tuplets – five babies	50	
Soixante	swah-sawnt	Link to six	60	
Soixante-dix	swah-sawnt-deese	Sixty-ten	70	
Soixante-et-onze	swah-sawnt-ay-awze	Sixty and eleven	71	
Soixante-douze	swah-sawnt-douhze	Sixty and twelve	72	
Quatre-vingts	kah-treuh-vah	Four twenties	80	
Quatre-vingt-un	kahtr-vah-ah	Four twenties one	81	
Quatre-vingt-dix	kahtr-vah-deese	Four twenties ten	90	
Quatre-vingt-onze	kahtr-vah-awze	Four twenties eleven	91	
Quatre-vingt-dix-neuf	kahtr-vah-deese-neuhff	Four twenties nine-teen	99	
Cent	saw	How many cents in a dollar? One hundred!	100	
Deux cents	deuh-saw		200	
Deux cent-un	deuh-saw-ah		201	
Mille	meal	There are a thousand Roman paces in a mile. A millipede has a thousand feet.	1,000	
Mille-un	meal-ah		1,001	
Dix mille	deese-meal		10,000	
Cent mille	saw-meal		100,000	
Un million	meal-yaw		million	
Un milliard	meal-yaahr	Sneaky! Where's Bill? The Bill of billion. He's gone to the mill.	billion	

Practise!

Write down the answer to the following sums, in French.

E.g. Quatre **fois** deux = douze

1. Trois fois dix = _____

2. Huit fois cinq = _____

3. Sept fois neuf = _____

E.g. Vingt-et-un **moins** un = vingt

4. Soixante moins six = _____

5. Mille moins cent = _____

6. Six moins un = _____

E.g. Soixante **plus** dix = soixante-dix

7. Cinquante plus deux = _____

8. Cent deux plus un = _____

9. Deux plus deux = _____

E.g. Douze **divisé par** quatre = trois

10. Cent divisé par deux = _____

11. Quatre divisé par un = _____

12. Zéro divisé par zero = _____

In each of the following write down, in French, a calculation that supplies the given answer. Use 'fois', 'moins', 'plus', 'divisé par' once each. E.g. Quatorze = dix plus quatre.

13. Soixante deux = _____

14. Vingt-quatre = _____

15. Vingt = _____

16. Quatre = _____

17. Make up your own calculations and write them down in French.

1. _____

2. _____

3. _____

4. _____

15: Les poids et les distances
[Weights and distances]

Word or phrase	Pronunciation guide	Aide-mémoire	English meaning	Check
Une bouteille de vin	oon bouh-tay-yeuh deuh vah	A **bu**tle**r** is the bottler, he uncorks the bottle, vin linked to w**in**e	A bottle of wine	
Une carafe d'eau	oon kah-raff doh	Eau – aqua, water	A carafe of water	
Un centimètre	ah sawn-tee-mett-reuh		A centimetre	
Un pied	ah pee-yay	**Ped**estrian, one who walks, **ped**, foot. A **pod**iatrist treats feet.	A foot	
Un pichet de rouge	ah pee-shay deuh rouh-zheuh	A **pi**t**che**r of red, a pitcher is a jug, linked to the pichet, glass container	A half-litre pitcher of wine	
Un kilomètre	ah kee-loh met-reuh		A kilometre	
Un litre	ah lee-treuh		A litre	
Un mètre	Ah met-reuh	A metre	A metre	
Un lot de cinq pommes	ah loh deuh sank paw	Un lot – a lot, a group, like a parking lot, for a group of cars	A pack of five apples	
Un quart de blanc	ah kaar deuh blaw	A quart is a quarter of a litre. Blank is generally white, white wine.	A quarter litre of white wine	
Un pouce	ah pousse	Also means thumb, earliest approx measure. An inch, you **pou**sh with your thumb.	An inch	
Proche/s		Ap**proach** means to get near	Close	
Les distances	lay dee-stoss		Distances	
Loin	lwah	**Lon**g way off	Far	
Un demi-kilo	ah dem-ee kee-loh	Demi is half. Demi-god, half-god. Demi-quaver in music, half quaver.	Half a kilo	
Un demi-litre	ah deuh-mee lee-treuh	Demi is half. Demi-god, half-god. Demi-quaver in music, half quaver.	Half a litre	
Lourd(e/s)	louhr/louhrd	This **loud** noise is heavy on my ea**r**s. Lord Lofty of Lourdes is a heavy lad!	Heavy	
Léger(s)/légère(s)	lay-zhay/lay-zhair	Linked to 'nég**ligé**', a **lig**ht night garment. Pizza liggera – light, less-fat pizza.	Light	
Près	pray	**Pr**ès, linked to **pr**oche, **near**ly the same, the words ap**pr**oach each other	Near	
Un kilo et demi	ah kee-loh ay deuh-mee		One and a half kilos	
Trois cents mètres	trwah saw mett-reuh	100 cents in a dollar. Trois cents – **thr**ee hundred, a **trio** is three.	Three hundred metres	
Une tonne	oon tawn		Ton	
Deux cents grammes	deuh saw gram		Two hundred grams	

Word or phrase	Pronunciation guide	Aide-mémoire	English meaning	Check
Deux cents mètres carrés	deuh saw mett-reuh kah-ray	**C**arr**é** linked to **qua**d**r**ant, (pronunciation of qua is 'kah'), quadrilateral, s**quare**	Two hundred square metres	
Deux kilos	deuh kee-loh		Two kilos	
Tout près	touh pray	**Tot**ally ap**pr**oached, very near	Very near	
Les poids	lay pwah	**Po**u**nds** and **po**u**nds** refers to weight, **po**rtly, heavy, **po**n**d**erou**s**, heavy-going	Weights	

Practise!

Guess the weights and measures of the following. Choose from the following five options:

deux litres
cinq centimètres
une tonne
quatre cents mètres
un pied

1. La longueur moyenne d'un pied. *(The average length of a foot.)*

   _____

2. Le poids d'une bouteille de lait qu'on achète le plus souvent.
   (The weight of a bottle of milk that is most often bought.)

   _____

3. La voiture de mon oncle. *(My uncle's car.)*

   _____

4. La longueur moyenne d'une oreille. *(The average length of an ear.)*

   _____

5. Le poids de la voiture de Jennifer. *(The weight of Jennifer's car.)*

   _____

16: Les opinions et les justifications
[Opinions and justifications]

Word or phrase	Pronunciation guide	Aide-mémoire	English meaning	Check
D'après	dah-pray	According to Daphne, 'Daddy, dab ray' was said by Dapper Dave.	According to	
Selon	seuh-law	According to Cyril, Cilla said 'So long!' before leaving!	According to	
Car	kaahr	**Car** links to f**or** when 'for' means 'because'. He drove it for it was his car!	Because	
Parce que	paahr-seuh-keuh	Parce que, parce que, parce que, because it **just is**!	Because	
Malgré	mal-gray	Malgré: gré – grace; mal – bad. Malgré le temps, il est sorti – Despite the weather, he went out. ('Malgré' means **not** accepting it **grace**fully). Therefore going out anyway, despite the conditions.	Despite	
Pour moi	pouhr mwah	P**our** – f**or**. Moi – me.	For me (in my opinion)	
Cependant	seuh-pawn-daw	Ce – this. Ce is in the phrase **c'est** – this is. Ce pendant – during this, 'given this', like however.	However	
Pourtant	pouhr-taw	Tant – so much. Ma tante fume tant – my aunt smokes so much. Pour (for) tant (so much) elle est athlète – However (for so much) she is an athlete.	However	
Je n'aime pas	zheuh nem pah	**N'** for negative, followed by pas. Aime – linked to amiable (likeable).	I don't like	
Je trouve	zheuh trouhv	Trouve – linked to trove. A treasure trove is a find, a discovery.	I find	
Je déteste	zheuh day-test	Je (I) **détest**e	I hate	
J'aime	zhem	Aime – linked to amiable (likeable)	I like	
Je l'aime	zheuh lem	Je l'aime literally means 'I it like'. Aime – linked to amiable (likeable).	I like it	
J'adore	zhah-dohr	J' (I) **adore** is closely linked to love	I love	
J'aime vraiment	zhem vray-maw	Aime – linked to amiable (likeable). Vraiment linked to **ver**i**t**able, real. Also, –ment, adverb, denotes, -ly.	I really like	
Je pense que	zheuh pawss keuh	If I am being **pens**ive, I am looking thoughtful, thinking	I think that	
Je crois que	zheuh krwah keuh	In**cre**dible means unbelievable. The **cre**ed is a recitation at church where you state belief.	I think (believe) that	
À mon avis	ah mawn ah-vee	'À mon avis' literally means 'To **m**y a**d**v**i**ce'. This is close to my opinion.	In my opinion	
Ça m'embête	sah mawm-bet	Bête – ê denotes 's' after e. Bête means beast. It me embeasts, turns me into a raging beast.	It annoys me	

Word or phrase	Pronunciation guide	Aide-mémoire	English meaning	Check
Ça me fait rire	sah meuh fay reer	'Ça me fait rire' literally means 'It me makes laugh'. **Fa**it – linked to **fa**bricate, manu**fa**cture, make. Rire – the verb, to laugh. You rear back when you laugh. Try it! Laugh heartily! See? You rear!	It makes me laugh	
Ça m'est égal	sah mate ay-gal	'Ça m'est égal' literally means 'It to me is **eq**ual', i.e. it is all the same to me.	It's all the same to me	
Peut-être que	peuh tet-reuh keuh	Peut comes from pouvoir, to be able (Pouvoir, power, ability). 'Peut être' – 'can be' or 'may be'. Peut-être que je peux avoir un 'A' en français – Maybe I can get an 'A' in French.	Maybe (followed by an idea)	
Si ça se trouve	see sah seuh trouhv	Literally means 'if it finds itself'. Maybe, if things find themselves like this. A treasure trove is a treasure find. Si ça se trouve, on gagnera – Maybe we'll win.	Maybe	
Moi non plus	mwah naw plooh	'Moi non plus' literally means 'me no more'. Non – no. Plus evokes more. 'Me no more [than you]' means, 'Me neither'.	Me neither	
Moi aussi	mwah oh-see	Aussi – **al**so. Both end with a vowel. Too and also are synonyms.	Me too	
Néanmoins	nay awe mwah	**Né**an**moins** – **Ne**verthe**less**. Moins – minus, less. 6 minus 5 is the same as 6 less 5, the answer is 1 for both.	Nevertheless	
D'une part	doon pahr	D'une part – of one part, on one hand	On one hand	
Au contraire	oh kawn-trair	On the **contrar**y	On the contrary	
Par contre	paahr kawn-treuh	Par – per, by. Contre, counter-attack, counter-argument. By the counter-argument.	On the other hand	
D'autre part	doat-reuh pahr	D'autre part – of other part, on the other hand. Autre and other are clearly linked.	On the other hand	
Peut-être	peuh-ett-reuh	Peut comes from pouvoir, to be able. (Pouvoir, power, ability). 'Peut être' means 'can be' or 'may be'.	Perhaps	
Personellement	pair saw nell-maw	-ment means -ly	Personally	
Ça ne me dit rien	sah neuh meuh dee ree-yeah	Literally means 'that to me says nothing'. **Di**t, **di**ction (**di**ctionary), words, say. Rien – nothing. In a famous song, 'Je ne regrette rien', I regret nothing. Also, 'De rien', (of nothing), Don't mention it, you're welcome!	That doesn't appeal to me	

Practise!

Translate the following into English:

1. Je crois que l'homme qui habite à la lune aime le fromage.

_____

2. Peut-être que je vais aller en ville le samedi.

_____

3. D'après mon père West Ham est une équipe terrible.

_____

4. À mon avis West Ham est la meilleure équipe anglaise.

_____

5. Le rugby, ça ne me dit rien, mais le tennis, je l'adore.

_____

6. D'une part, j'aime l'école. D'autre part, c'est stressant.

_____

7. Si ça se trouve, la planète Mars est habitable.

_____

8. Ça m'est égal si Liverpool gagne la ligue.

_____

9. J'ai mangé tout le chocolat malgré mes meilleures intentions.

_____

10. C'est difficile. Néanmoins, je vais essayer!

_____

Translate the following into French:

11. I really like going to the cinema.

_____

12. "I don't like cheese!", "Me neither!"

_____

13. "I love it!", "Me too!"

_____

14. I hate working!

_____

15. It annoys me when I cry.

_____

17: Les prépositions
(Prepositions)

Word or phrase	Pronunciation guide	Aide-mémoire	English meaning	Check
environ	awe-vee-raw	Your **environ**ment is what is around and **about** you	About (quantity)	
Vers	vair	A 'revers' is a setback, a reverse from where you want to be. The opposite, 'vers', is towards. Il arrive vers midi – he is coming towards (around) midday.	About (time) towards	
Au dessus de	oh deuh-sooh deuh	Au des**su**s de – includes 'su' which is used in **su**perior, meaning above.	Above	
Selon	seuh-law	According to ze-law, Ceylon is called Sri Lanka.	According to	
Contre	kawn-treuh	Counter-attack is an attack back **against** one's adversary.	Against	
Parmi	paahr-mee	'Pour moi, Paris est **parmi** les plus belles villes du monde' – For me, Paris is **among** the most beautiful cities in the world. Are **parm**a violets **among** your favourite sweets?	Among	
Autour de	oh-touhr deuh	I decided to do a **tour around** the castle	Around (e.g. the castle) outside it	
Alentours, aux alentours de	ah-lawn-touhr, oze, ah-lawn-touhr deuh	Alen**tours** suggests a **tour**, which suggests going **around** an area. Aux alentours de Paris – around (close to) Paris.	Around (vicinity of)	
À	ah	À la maison – at home. De A à B – from A to B; à Belfast – in Belfast.	At/to/in	
Chez	shay	Chez moi – at my house. Chez nous – At our house. Chez McDo – at McDonald's. Chez Shay – at Shay's.	At (someone's)	
Au fond de	oh faw deuh	The **found**ations are found at the bottom of the building	At the back of/ bottom of	
Au bord de	oh bohr deuh	On the **bord**er is at the side or the edge of another area	At the edge/ side of	
Au bord duquel	oh bohr doo-kell	'Le parc au bord duquel je vis' – The park I live beside. (de + le = duquel, de + la = de laquelle, de + les = desquels/desquelles)	At the edge of which	
Avant	ah-vaw	**A**d**van**ce parties go before the rest	Before	
Derrière	dair-ee-air	At the **re**a**r**, at de-rear (derrière), behind	Behind	
Sous	souh	Sous, a sous chef is below the chef. **Sou**s-marin – sub marine, under water.	Below	
Au dessous de	oh deuh-souh deuh	Des**sous**, sous means 'under' and that is our link.	Below, beneath, underneath	
À côté de	ah koh-tay deuh	ô denotes 's' after the o. La côte is the coast, the sea-**side**.	Beside	

Word or phrase	Pronunciation guide	Aide-mémoire	English meaning	Check
Entre	awe-treuh	E**ntre** – I**nter**. Between nations, **inter**national. **Inter**vene, to come (vene) between.	Between	
Au-delà de	oh deuh-lah deuh	Yodela deuh-euh. Yodela deuh-euh. Say it. You'll sound like a yodeler, yodeling beyond the mountains.	Beyond	
Bas, en bas de	bah, awe bah de	A **bas**e note is a low note	Bottom, at the bottom of	
Par	paahr	**Par** avion – by airmail. Par exemple – by example.	By	
Près de	pray deuh	**Pr**ès de linked to 'ap**pr**oach', linked to **pr**oche, near, close to close	Close, near	
En dépit de	awe day-pee deuh	Dépit – **de**s**pit**e	Despite	
Pendant	pawn-daw	While the **pend**ulum swings. During the swinging of the **pend**ulum.	During	
Loin	lwaah deuh	Loin de – pronounced like **L**(R)**wanda**, which is a country that is loin (far) de (from) the British Isles.	Far	
Loin de	lwaah deuh	Loin de, a **lon**g way from, **far** from	Far from	
Pour	pouhr	P**our** – F**or**	For	
De	deuh	De A à B – From A to B	From	
Haut, en haut de	oh, awe oh deuh	**H**igh, **alt**i**tu**de, **hau**gh**t**y describes one who holds self above others	High/top of	
En	awe	En – in	In (in an abstract way)	
Dans, dans un	daw, dawze ah	In Dan's den. Dan's in debt to an insider.	In, in a	
Devant	deuh-vaw	The ad**van**ce party goes in front of the rest. At the **van**guard – at the front.	In front of	
Lieu, au lieu de	lyeuh, oh lyeuh deuh	Time off in **lieu** (stead) of pay. **Lieu**tenant holds the place (lieu), tenant holding the lease. **Tena**cious describes one who won't let go. Who will hold.	Instead of/in place of	
Malgré	mahl-gray	**Gr**é linked to **gr**ace. Il a agi de bon gré – He acted in good grace. Il a agi malgré – He acted in bad grace, i.e. against a desire or against someone's wishes, which is the meaning of 'in spite of'.	In spite of	
Milieu, au milieu de	mee-lyeuh, oh mee-lyeuh deuh	**Mi**ddle, **mi**dnight, **mi**dday, **mi**lieu, middle of place, in a certain milieu, middle of group	Middle of	
Près de	pray deuh	In the **pre**cinct means it is close by. Something in my **pres**ence is close to me.	Near, close	
Proche de	prosh deuh	To approach is to go near or close (proche)	Near, close	

Word or phrase	Pronunciation guide	Aide-mémoire	English meaning	Check
De	deuh	Joie **de** vivre – joy **of** living. Crème de la crème – cream of the cream. Tour de France – Tour of France.	Of/from	
Sur	soohr	Sir is above the rest. S**ur**name is above your first name in importance. Sur without ^ means 'on'.	On	
En face de	awe fass deuh	Facing is opposite, e.g. in a block a flats, the flat that is facing mine is opposite mine.	Opposite	
Dehors, en dehors de	awe deuh-oar deuh	Literally 'de hors' – 'of out(side)'. Hors service – out of service.	Outside, outside of	
Droit devant	drwah deuh-vaw	D**roit** – **ri**ght. 'Dieu et mon droit!' – God and my right – this is the British Royal motto. De va**nt** – in fro**nt**.	Right in front	
Sûr de	soohr deuh	Sûr – sure	Sure of	
À travers	ah trah-vair	To **traverse** the Great Plain is to go **through** the Great Plain	Through	
À	ah	**Le** concert **auquel** je vais. The concert I go to. (à + **le** = **auquel**, à + laquelle = à la, à + les = auxquels/auxquelles)	To	
À gauche de	ah gohsh deuh	Gauche is a word found in English, meaning clumsy, not appropriate. Like the expression, 'up the left'!	To the left of	
À droite de	ah drwaat deuh	D**roit**e is the direction 'right'. Linked to d**roit**, meaning, one's **ri**ght to act. 'Dieu et mon droit' – 'God and my right'.	To the right of	
Haut, en haut de	oh, awe oh deuh	**H**igh, **al**ti**tu**de, **hau**gh**t**y describes one who holds self above others	Top (high)/ on top of	
Envers	awe-vair	Envers – almost the opposite of revers. Un revers is a **setback**, a reverse. Therefore an envers is a **setforward**. The word setforward doesn't exist but it suggests, 'towards'.	Towards	
Sous	souh	**So**us – **su**b-marine means under the water	Under	
Jusqu à	zhoose kah	Jus**qu**'à – up to (qu – up). Just up to or until.	Until	
Jusqu'à ce que	zhoose kass keuh	Jus**qu**'à – up to (qu – up). Just up to or until.	Until + phrase	
Jusqu'à	zhoose-kah	Jus**qu**'à – up to (qu – up). Just up to or until.	Up to	
Avec	ah-vek	Avec moi – with me. Avec Alek – with Alek.	With	
Sans	saw	Sans – Médecins Sans Frontières. (Doctors **Without** Borders). Sans doute, without doubt.	Without (any) doubt	

Practise!

Fais un dessin pour chacune de ces phrases *(Draw a picture for each of these phrases)*.

1. Le chat est droit devant la voiture.

2. L'oiseau est sur la branche.

3. Le serpent est derrière ma sœur.

4. La voiture est sous l'éléphant.

18: Les pronoms
(Pronouns)

Word or phrase	Pronunciation guide	Example of usage	English meaning	Check
Me	meuh	Je me lave – I wash myself. Il me parle – He speaks to me. Je me chante – I sing to myself.	Me, myself, to me, to myself	
Te	teuh	Tu te laves – you wash yourself. Il te parle – He speaks to you. Tu te chantes – you sing to yourself.	You (singular), yourself, to you (singular), to yourself	
La	lah	Je la vois – I see her. Elle la voit – She sees it.	Her/it (f)	
Lui	loo-wee	Je lui parle – I speak to her. il lui parle – he speaks to it.	To her/to it (indirect pronoun)	
Le	leuh	Je le vois – I see him. Elle le déteste – She hates it.	Him/it (m)	
Lui	loo-wee	Il lui parle – He speaks to him. Elle lui parle – She speaks to it.	To him/to it (indirect pronoun)	
Se	seuh	Il se voit – He sees himself. Il se parle – He speaks to himself. Le chien se voit – The dog sees itself.	Himself, to himself, herself, to herself, itself, to itself	
Le, la	leuh, lah	Elle le prend – She takes it. Il la mange – He eats it.	It/him, it/her	
En	awe	Tu parles de l'école > Tu **en** parles – You talk about it. Il en connaît trois – He knows three of them.	Of (about) it, of (about) them. (En replaces de + noun)	
Y, là	ee, lah	Il y mange – He eats there. Il habite là – He lives there. Il pense à l'argent (Il y pense) – He thinks about the money (He thinks about it).	There ('Y' replaces à + noun), there	
Nous	nouh	Ils nous aiment – They like us. Nous nous aimons – we like ourselves. Elle nous parle – she speaks to us.	Us, to us, ourselves, to ourselves	
Vous	vouh	Ils vous aiment – They like you. Vous vous aimez – you like yourselves. Il vous parle – he speaks to you.	You (pl), to you (pl), yourselves, to yourselves	
Les	lay	Nous les aimons – We like them. Je les aime – I like them.	Them	
Leur	leuhr	On leur parle – We (one) speak to them.	To them (indirect pronoun)	
Se	seuh	Elles se lavent – They wash themselves. Elles se parlent – They speak to each other.	Themselves (m/f), to themselves (m/f)	

Practise!

Match the following French sentences to the correct English translation. The first one has been done for you.

1.	Il me voit	**G**	**A.**	I saw you (pl)	
2.	Ils les comprennent		**B.**	He saw her	
3.	Est-ce que tu les connaîs?		**C.**	She washes herself every morning	
4.	Je vous ai vus		**D.**	He went there	
5.	Elle nous a parlé		**E.**	She studied there	
6.	On leur parle chaque jour		**F.**	You (formal) spoke to her	
7.	Il l'a vue		**G.**	He sees me	
8.	Je lui ai parlé		**H.**	They understand them	
9.	Elle se lave tous les matins		**I.**	She spoke to us	
10.	Il y est allé		**J.**	Do you (informal) know them?	
11.	Elle y a étudié		**K.**	We (one) speak to them every day	
12.	Ils se parlent tous les jours		**L.**	I spoke to him	
13.	Elle se connaîssent depuis l'école primaire		**M.**	They speak to each other every day	
14.	On en parle chaque jour		**N.**	They've known each other since primary school	
15.	On en a parlé hier		**O.**	I gave it to him	
16.	Je la lui ai donnée		**P.**	We know each other	
17.	Nous nous connaîssons		**Q.**	We (one) speak about it every day	
18.	Vous lui avez parlé		**R.**	We (one) spoke about it yesterday	

19: Les pronoms après les prépositions
(Pronouns after prepositions)

Word or phrase	Pronunciation guide	Example of usage	English meaning	Check
Elle	el	Je vis près d'elle – I live near her. Il voyage sans elle – He travels without her.	Her, it	
Elle-même	el-mem	Elle discute avec elle-même – She is discussing with herself	Herself, itself	
Lui	loo-wee	Est-ce que tu travailles sans lui? – Do you work without him?	Him, it	
Lui-même	loo-wee-mem	Il est fâché contre lui-même – He is angry against himself	Himself, itself	
Moi	mwah	Moi – me. Viens avec moi s'il te plait – Come with me please.	Me	
Moi-même	mwah-mem	Je travaille pour moi-même – I work for myself	Myself	
Soi	swah	On doit penser à soi – One must think of one(self)	One	
Soi-même	swah-mem	Il est difficile d'être loin de soi-même – It is difficult to be far from oneself	Oneself	
Elles	el	Elles habitent près d'elles – They live near them	Them (f)	
Elles-mêmes	el-mem	Elles sont fâchées contre elles-mêmes – They are annoyed at themselves	Themselves (fpl)	
Eux	euh	Je ne vais pas partir sans eux – I am not going to leave without them	Them (m)	
Eux-mêmes	euh-mem	Ils ont pensé à eux-mêmes – They thought to (of) themselves	Themselves (mpl)	
Nous	nouh	Ils vont rester avec nous – They are going to stay with us	Us	
Nous-mêmes	nouh-mem	Nous sommes sûrs de nous-mêmes – We are sure of ourselves	Ourselves	
Toi	twah	Je déteste être loin de toi – I hate being far from you	You (s)	
Toi-même	twah-mem	Tu es pour toi-même – You are for yourself	Yourself	
Vous	vouh	Je ne vais pas aller avec vous – I am not going to go with you	You (pl)	
Vous-mêmes	vouh-mem	Vous êtes contre vous-mêmes – You are against yourselves	Yourselves	

Practise!

Match the following French sentences to the correct English translation. The first one has been done for you.

1. Je sors avec elle **F**

2. Il va sans moi

3. Tu l'as fait derrière moi

4. Elle l'a vu avec elle

5. Il s'est assis à côté de moi

6. Elle était assise loin de nous

7. Je suis très proche d'elle

8. En face de vous, il y a un gangster

9. Les soeurs le font pour elles-mêmes

10. Je travaille pour eux

11. Ils vivent près d'elle

12. On regarde autour de soi

13. Il cherche dans lui-même

14. Il est contre toi

15. Nous allons vers eux

16. Ils vivent au-dessus de nous

17. Elles vivent au-dessous d'eux

A. They live near her

B. They live above us

C. I work for them

D. Sisters are doing it for themselves

E. They live under them

F. I am going out with her

G. She saw him with her

H. He sat down beside me

I. He is going without me

J. You did it behind me

K. He is searching in himself

L. We (one) are looking around ourselves

M. Opposite you there is a gangster

N. She was sitting far from us

O. I am very close to her

P. We are going towards them

Q. He is against you

20: Les questions
(Questions)

Word or phrase	Pronunciation guide	Aide-mémoire	English meaning	Check
Quelle heure?	ah kell euhr	At which hour (heure). À (**At**) quelle (kell the **whitch**) heure (hour-time). À quelle heure? – At which time?	At which time?	
Depuis combien de temps?	kawm-bee-yen deuh taw	Since how much of time, **tem**ps. 'Tempus fugit' is Latin for 'time flies'.	For (Since) how long?	
D'où?	douh	De – of/from. Crème **de** la crème – cream **from/of** the cream. Where do you see it? Right on top of the u – ù! D'où – from where.	From/of where?	
Comment?	kaw-maw	Addressing a magician: '**Commaw**, **how** did you do it?'	How?	
Comment ça s'écrit?	kaw-maw sah say-kree	'**Commaw**, **how** did you do it?' Comment (how) ça s'écrit (it writes itself) – How it writes itself? (écrire – to write. é at the start of a word replaces 's'. **scri**be, **scri**pt.)	How is that written?	
Combien (de)?	kawm-bee-yen	How much **combin**g do you do in the morning?	How many/ much?	
C'est combien, ça?	say kawm-bee-yen, sah	C'est – It **is** combien (how much **combin**g do you do?) It is how much, that?	How much is that?	
Combien est-ce que c'est?	kawm-bee-yen ess-keuh say	How much **combin**g do you do in the morning? Combien est-ce que (is it that) c'**es**t (it **is**)?	How much is that? (more formally)	
Est-ce que c'est un problème?	ess-keuh say ah prob-lem	Est-ce que – Is it that. C'**es**t – it **is**. Un problème – a problem.	Is it a problem?	
Est-ce que?	ess-keuh	**Es**t = is. Ce – it. Que – that.	Is it that?	
Questions	kess-tee-awe		Questions	
Que?	keuh	In French, '**Que** sera sera!' – **What**ever will be, will be!	What?	
Quoi?	kwah	Quoi is a more abrupt, what? Found in the question, **P**our quoi? (**for** what? = why?)	What? (not followed by a phrase)	
C'est de quelle couleur?	say deuh kell kouh-leuhr	C'est – it is. **De** – of (Tour **de** France – Tour **of** France). Quelle – which **col**our. (Literally, 'It is of which colour?')	What (which) colour is it?	
Quelle est la date?	kell ay la daht	Quelle – which (Kell the whitch). **Es**t – **is**. La date – the date.	What (which) date is it?	
Quel jour est-il?	kell jouhr ate-eel	Quel – **which**; jour – day (bonjour = good **day**); **es**t – **is**; **il** – **it**? (il means it/he)	What (which) day is it?	

Word or phrase	Pronunciation guide	Aide-mémoire	English meaning	Check
Qu'est-ce **que** tu aimes?	kess-keuh-tooh em	In French, '**Qu(e)** sera sera!' means '**what**ever will be, will be!' Qu' (what) est-ce que – is it that. Tu aimes – you like. What is it that you like? (aimer – to like, love; amiable – likeable; Amy, Aimée – girl's name, 'loved one').	What do you like? (What is it that you like?)	
Qu'est-ce qui se passe?	kess-kee-seuh pass	In French, '**Qu(e)** sera sera!' means '**What**ever will be, will be!' Qu' (what) est-ce qui – is it that. Se passe – is happening. What is it that is happening? (se passer – to happen, like come to **pass**; what is happening? = what is coming to pass?)	What is happening? (what is it that is happening)	
Quelle heure est-il?	kell euhr ate-eel	Quelle – **which** (Kell the whitch). Heure – **hour**.	What (which) time is it?	
Qu'est-ce qui ne va pas?	kess-kee-neuh vah pah	In French, '**Qu(e)** sera sera!' means '**What**ever will be, will be!' Qu(e)'est-ce (what is it) qui (that) ne (not – **ne**gative) va (going – vavavoom) pas?	What is wrong? (What is not going?)	
Quel temps fait-il?	kell taw fate-eel	**Temp**s – **temp**erature, linked to the weather	What's (which) the weather like?	
Où?	ooh	Where? Right on top of the 'u', ù! Where d**o ù** see it?	Where?	
Quand?	kaw	The only one with the 'n' of whe**n**. 'Tell me when will you be mine? Tell me cuando, cuando cuando.' A song by Englebert Humperdinck. Cuando is Spanish, it's like quand.	When?	
Quel(s)/ Quelle(s)	kell	'Quell the revolution started by that whitch!' Or just kell (Quel) the witch!	Which?	
Avec qui?	ah-vek kee	Who is the **key (qui)** to the question?	With whom?	
Qui?	key	Who is **key (qui)** to the question?	Who?	
Pourquoi?	pour-kwah	Quoi – linked to que, another word for what. 'For (p**our**) what?' means 'why'?	Why?	

Practise!

Match the questions below to the correct response. The first one has been done for you.

Questions

1. Où vas-tu?   **B**

2. Avec qui est-ce que tu vas aller?

3. C'est de quelle couleur votre voiture?

4. Combien de personnes y-a-t il en France

5. Où as-tu mis mon stylo?

6. Quand viens-tu à la fête?

7. Est-ce que c'est important de parler portugais?

8. Quelle fille l'a fait?

9. Quel temps fait-il?

10. Quelle heure est-il?

11. Qu'est-ce qui se passe?

12. Depuis combien de temps tu le connaîs?

13. D'où viens-tu?

14. Comment vas-tu?

15. Comment ça s'écrit?

16. Quelle est la date de ton anniversaire?

17. Pourquoi est-ce que tu l'as fait?

18. Qu'est-ce qui est arrivé?

Les réponses (answers)

A. Oui, c'est très important de le parler

B. Je vais aller avec mon frère

C. Il fait chaud mais il pleut

D. Ma voiture est verte

E. Je vais en ville

F. Il y en a 66 millions à peu près

G. C'est le quatre février

H. Parce que je voulais le faire

I. Ça s'écrit Bay Ah Tay

J. Je l'ai mis dans ma trousse

K. Je viens à huit heures

L. Christine l'a fait

M. Il est huit heures dix

N. Je viens de Belfast

O. Je le connaîs depuis deux ans

P. Rien, rien du tout

Q. Je vais très bien merci

R. La voiture est tombée en panne

21: L'heure, Quelle heure est-il?, Il est huit heures!
(Time, Which time is it?, It is eight o'clock!)

Word or phrase	Pronunciation guide	Aide-mémoire	English meaning	Check
Pendant la matinée	pawn-daw lah mah-tee-nay	While the **pend**ulum swings (during). La matinee (early) showing, morning.	During the morning	
Pendant la journée	pawn-daw lah jouhr-nay	While the **pend**ulum swings (during). Journée – keep a daily **journ**al.	During the day	
Pendant la soirée	pawn-daw lah swah-ray	While the **pend**ulum swings (during). A soirée is a fancy evening party.	During the evening	
Le soir (m)	leuh swaahr	Soir, soirée, evening	Evening (in the)	
l'après-midi	lap-pray-mee-dee	**A**p**r**è**s** – **af**t**er**. Midi – midday, noon. (Après-ski – after skiing.)	In the afternoon	
Le jour	leuh jour	Jour – keep a daily **jour**nal. The **jour**nalist works for a daily newspaper.	In the day	
Le soir	leuh swaahr	A **soir**ée is a fancy evening out.	In the evening	
le matin	leuh mah-tah	Matinee – morning (early) showing, morning	In the morning	
Est-il?	ate-eel	**Es**t-il – **Is** it	Is it?	
Il est une heure	eel ate oon euhrr	U**ne** – o**ne** hour	It is 1 o'clock	
Il est une heure cinq	eel ate oon euhrr sank	U**ne** – o**ne** hour. C**in**q – five, qu**in**tuplets.	It is 1:05	
Il est une heure dix	eel ate oon euhrr deese	U**ne** – o**ne** hour. Dix – ten, decimal, dice.	It is 1:10	
Il est une heure quinze	eel ate oon euhrr kahzz	U**ne** – o**ne** hour. Quinze (**quin**tuplet – link to five, fifteen).	It is 1:15	
Il est une heure et quart	eel ate oon euhrr ay kaahr	U**ne** – o**ne** hour. Quart – quarter.	It is a quarter past one	
Il est une heure vingt	eel ate oon euhrr vant	U**ne** – o**ne** hour. Vingt – t**w**e**nt**y, the 'nt' sound is common to both.	It is twenty past one	
Il est une heure vingt-cinq	eel ate oon euhrr vant-sank	U**ne** – o**ne** hour. Vingt – t**w**e**nt**y, the 'nt' sound is common. C**in**q – five, qu**in**tuplets.	It is twenty-five past one	
Il est une heure trente	eel ate oon euhrr trawnt	U**ne** – o**ne** hour. **T**ren**te** – **t**hir**t**y.	It is one thirty	
Il est une heure et demie	eel ate oon euhrr ay deuh-mee	U**ne** – o**ne** hour. Demie – a demigod is a half-god.	It is half one	
Il est deux heures moins vingt-cinq	eel ay deuhz euhrr mwah vant-sank	**Due**t links to deux (two). Heures – hours. Moins – minus (minus vingt-cinq).	It is twenty-five to two	
Il est deux heures moins vingt	eel ay deuhz euhrr mwah vant	**Due**t link to deux (two). Heures – hours. Moins – minus (minus vingt).	It is twenty to two	
Il est deux heures moins le quart	eel ay deuhz euhrr mwah leuh kaahr	**Due**t link to deux (two). Heures – hours. Moins – minus. Le quart – the quarter.	It is a quarter to two	

Word or phrase	Pronunciation guide	Aide-mémoire	English meaning	Check
Il est deux heures moins dix	eel ay deuhz euhrr mwah deese	**Due**t link to deux (two). Heures – hours. Moins – minus (minus dix – decimal – ten).	It is ten to two	
Il est deux heures moins cinq	eel ay deuhz euhrr mwah sank	**Due**t link to deux (two). Heures – hours. Moins – minus (minus cinq – qu**in**tuplets).	It is five to two	
Il est deux heures	eel ay deuhz euhrr	**Due**t link to deux (two). Heures – hours.	It is 2 o'clock	
Il est deux heures cinq	eel ay deuhz euhrr sank	**Due**t link to deux (two). Heures – hours. Cinq (qu**in**tuplets).	It is 2:05	
Il est deux heures dix	eel ay deuhz euhrr deese	**Due**t link to deux (two). Heures – hours. Dix (decimal – 10)	It is 2:10	
Il est deux heures et quart	eel ay deuhz euhrr ay kaahr	**Due**t link to deux (two). Heures – hours. et (and) quart (quarter).	It is a quarter past 2	
Il est 2 heures vingt	eel ay deuhz euhrr vant	**Due**t link to deux (two). Heures – hours. Vingt – t**went**y, note 'nt' sound – twe**nt**y.	It is 2:20	
Il est 2 heures vingt-cinq	eel ay deuhz euhrr vant-sank	**Due**t link to deux (two). Heures – hours. Vingt-cinq.	It is 2:25	
Il est 2 heures et demie	eel ay deuhz euhrr ay deuh-mee	Demie like semi. A demigod is a half-god.	It is half 2	
Il est 3 heures moins vingt-cinq	eel ay trwazz euhrr mwah vant-sank	Trio – link to trois (three) moins (minus) vingt-cinq	It is 25 to 3	
Il est 3 heures moins vingt	eel ay trwazz euhrr mwah vant	Trio – link to trois (three) moins (minus) vingt	It is 20 to 3	
Il est 3 heures moins le quart	eel ay trwazz euhrr mwah leuh kaahr	Moins – minus. Moins le quart – less the quarter. 3 heures minus the quarter.	It is a quarter to 3	
Il est minuit	mean-wee	Mi – middle. Nuit – night.	It is midnight	
Il est midi	eel ay mee-dee	Midi – midday. Remember, di = day, lun-di etc. Mid (mi) day (di) = midi – midday.	It is noon	
Il est treize heures	eel ay trezz euhrr	**Tr**ei**z**e (**t**hi**r**tee**n**), we have the idea of trio but it is a longer word than trois.	It is 13 hundred hours	
Il est treize heures cinq	eel ay trezz euhrr sank	**Tr**ei**z**e (**t**hi**r**tee**n**), we have the idea of trio but it is a longer word than trois.	It is 13:05	
Il est treize heures dix	eel ay trezz euhrr deese	**Tr**ei**z**e (**t**hi**r**tee**n**), we have the idea of trio but it is a longer word than trois.	It is 13:10	
Il est treize heures quinze	eel ay trezz euhrr kahzz	**Tr**ei**z**e (**t**hi**r**tee**n**), we have the idea of trio but it is a longer word than trois.	It is 13:15	
Il est treize heures trente	eel ay trezz euhrr trawnt	**Tr**ei**z**e (**t**hi**r**tee**n**), we have the idea of trio but it is a longer word than trois.	It is 13:30	
Il est treize heures quarante-cinq	eel ay trezz euhrr kah-rawnt sank	**Tr**ei**z**e (**t**hi**r**tee**n**). **Qua**rante – cinq (quad, four), quarante, longer than quatre.	It is 13:45	
La nuit (f)	lah nwee	Nocturnal – **n**u**i**t	Night (at)	
Quel(le/s) Heure (f) est-il?	Kell euhrr ay-teel	'Kell the which!' sorry witch, it's for vocabulary learning purposes. **H**e**u**r**e** – **h**o**ur**.	What (which) time is it?	

Practise!

Use the daily routine phrases below to chart your daily routine with times. Write the phrases and times out in words in French using both the 12 hour clock and the 24 hour clock. Two have been done for you.

Je me lève à   Je quitte la maison à   Je me couche à
L'école commence à   J'arrive à l'école à   Je prends mon dîner à
Je mange le petit-déjeuner à   Je rentre à

Anglais (English)	Anglais (English)	Français (French)
I wake up at:	7.30 am	*Je me réveille à **sept heures et demie.***
		*Je me réveille à **sept heures trente.***
I get up at:	_____	
I eat breakfast at:	_____	
I leave the house at:	_____	
I arrive in school at:	_____	
School starts at:	_____	
School finishes at:	3.25 pm	*L'école se termine à **trois heures vingt-cinq.***
		*L'école se termine à **quinze heures vingt-cinq.***
I get home at:	_____	
I have my dinner at:	_____	
I go to bed at:	_____	

22: Expressions of time
[Expressions du temps]

Word or phrase	Pronunciation guide	Aide-mémoire	English meaning	Check
Jour (m)	jouhr	Bon-**jour** – good-day	A day	
Une journée (f)	oon zhouhr-nay	A **journ**al is a daily record of what one does	A day	
Une quinzaine (f)	oon kaaz-en	Quinze, **quin**tuplets, five (not fifteen babies). The 'aine' is like 'ish'. Therefore quinzaine = fifteen**ish** days.	A fortnight	
À tout à l'heure	ah touh tah leuhr	To do with time, because of the hour, heure	A while ago/ in a while	
Après	ah-pray	**A prey** is held by a bird of prey **after** the hunt. Après-ski – after skiing, après-midi – after noon.	After	
Après-demain	ah-pray deuh-mah	Après – **af**t**er**s, there is a clear link! De main day is tomorrow. We can't change the present and the past is gone!	After tomorrow	
Encore	awe-core	What we say for 'again' at a concert	Again	
Tout le temps	tou leuh taw	**Tot**ality of **tim**e, all the time	All the time	
Toujours	tou-zhouhr	Tou (from total, all), jour from bon-jour, good-day, all the days, always	Always	
Vers 8 heures	vair weet euhr	**Veer**ing towards, is locating close to something. Towards or around a given time.	Around 8 o'clock	
À la dernière minute	ah lah dair-nee-air mee-noot	Dernière – last. Opposite of première, first.	At the last minute	
Avant	ah-vaw	An **ad**va**n**ce party is a group that goes **before** the others.	Before	
Avant-hier	ah-vawnt-yair	The **ad**va**n**ce party, before the rest. Hi**er** pronounced 'yair', The pronunciation is linked to **y**est**er**day.	Before yesterday	
En retard	awe reuh-taahr	Retarded is held back, delayed	Delayed	
Pendant longtemps	pawn-daw long-taw	A pendulum, something that keeps swinging on a grand-father clock, **during** a long temps – long time.	During a long time	
Chaque jour	shaak-zhouhr	**Cha**que has all the letters of 'each', just backwards.	Each day	
Tôt	toh	Little **tot**s are **early** learners	Early	
De bonne heure	deuh bawn euhr	Of good hour (de bonne heure). Remember, (**bon**-jour = **good** day)	Early	
Un soir	ah swaahr	In English, a soirée means a social gathering in the evening	Evening	
Une soirée (f)	oon swah-ray	In English, a soirée means a social gathering in the evening	Evening	
Tous les jours	touh-lay-zhouhr	Total the days, all the days, every day	Every day	
Pendant trois jours	pawn-daw trwah jouhr	A pendulum, something that keeps swinging on a grand-father clock, during (for) three (**trio**) days (bon-**jour** – good-**day**).	For three days	

Word or phrase	Pronunciation guide	Aide-mémoire	English meaning	Check
De temps de temps	deuh tawze awe taw	Temps linked to time	From time to time	
Tout de suite	touht sweet	A **suit**or is a follower of a lady, **tot**ally following, straight away, immediately	Immediately	
Aussitôt	oh-see-toh	**Au**ssi. Tôt – early. O denotes an 's' after the o. **To**ast, for **early** morning. As early as possible is immediately.	Immediately	
Tard	taahr	If you are tardy in English, you are late	Late	
Un mois m	ah mwah	**Mo**nth	Month (one)	
Un matin	ah mat-ah	Matinée is an early showing at the cinema. There used to be a morning showing, 'Frère Jacques, sonnez les matines!' means 'Brother John, ring the morning bells!'	Morning	
Une matinée (f)	mat-ee-nay	Matinée is an early showing. At the cinema, used to be a morning showing.	Morning	
Plus ou moins	plooh-zoh-mwah	Plus – more. Moins – minus, less.	More or less	
Jamais	zhah-may	Je ne mange jamais de la confiture – I never eat **jam**	Never	
Normalement	nohr-mahl-maw		Normally	
Pas du tout	pah dou tou	'Pah' is an offhand negative remark. Du tout – of total, of all. Hence pas de tour – not at all.	Not at all	
Souvent	souh-vaw	Souvent, look at the letters, **ovten**, is in there!	Often	
Une fois	oon fwah	Il était une fois – once upon a time. Trois fois – three times.	Once	
À temps		Like **at** **tim**e which is like 'on time'	On time	
Récemment	ray-say-maw		Recently	
Dernièrement	dair-nee-air-maw	Dernière – opposite of première, first. The -ment denotes 'ly'.	Recently	
À tout à l'heure	ah touh tah leuhr	**Toodle** pip is an old-fashioned way of saying 'see ya', it is linked to **tout à l'**heure.	See you soon	
Quelques jours	kell-keuh jouhr	Qu**e**lque**s** – **s**om**e**? At least we have a common 'e' and a common 's'. Some kelkeuh please! 'Kelkeuh' is Russian honeycomb, maybe.	Some days	
Parfois	paahr-fwah	Par – by. Par avion – by air(mail), by times, sometimes.	Sometimes	
Par moments	paahr moh-maw	By moments is sometimes	Sometimes	
Tantôt...tantôt...	tawn-toh... tawn-toh...	**T**an**t**ô**t** **t**an**t**ô**t** sounds a little like from **t**ime to **t**ime. Il est tantôt triste, tantôt heureux – he is sometimes sad, sometimes happy.	Sometimes X Sometimes Y	
Tantôt	tawn-toh	Tant – so much. Tôt – early. Ma tante fume **tant** – my aunt smokes **so much**. The ô denotes 's' after the o. **To**ast is **early** morning food. A combination of so much and early = soon.	Soon	

Word or phrase	Pronunciation guide	Aide-mémoire	English meaning	Check
Toujours	touh-zhouhr	Tou – from total, all. Jour – from bon-jour, good-day. All the days, always, leads to still (all the time, days).	Still (continuous)	
Les vacances d'été	lay vah-kawse day-tay	Vacation, holiday. Été – 'estival' means summery in French. F**estival** is a combination of this and party (fête).	Summer holidays	
Les grandes vacances (f)	les grawnd vah-kawse	Grandes – tall, long vacations – the summer ones	Summer holidays	
Le lendemain (m)	leuh lawn-deuh-mah	The longdemain is the day after, the long tomorrow.	The day after	
La première fois	lah preuh-mee-yair fwah	Premier League is the first league. Fois – time (une fois, deux fois, trois fois).	The first time	
La dernière fois	lah dair-nyair fwah	**De**adline, opposite of prem**ier**, dern**ier**. Fois – time (une fois, deux fois, trois fois).	The last time	
Le jour suivant (m)	leuh jouhr swee-vaw	En suite, next to bedroom. Jour – day, bon jour, good day. **Sui**vant – next day.	The next day	
Le temps	leuh taw	'Tempus fugit' is Latin for 'time flies'. Temporary – part-time, looks like **time**.	Time (general)	
Aujourd'hui	oh-zheuhr-dwee	Au – at the. Jour – day, like bonjour – good day. 'Hui' is from Latin 'hodie', today. French literally means 'at the day of today'.	Today	
Demain	deuh-mah	De main day is tomorrow. We can't change the present and the past is gone!	Tomorrow	
Une semaine (f)	oon seuh-men	**Se**ven days **se**maine	Week (one)	
Hier	ee-yair	Hi**er** is pronounced 'yair'. This pronunciation links to yest**er**day.	Yesterday	

Practise!

Translate the following into French:

1. I play football during the Summer holidays. _____

_____

2. Yesterday, I did my homework for today. _____

_____

3. I arrived late the day before yesterday. _____

_____

4. The first time that I went to the cinema. _____

_____

5. I eat chocolate all the time. _____

_____